GRAND CANYON COUNTRY

GRAND CANYON NATIONAL PARK OAK CREEK – SEDONA
GRAND CANYON CAVERNS WUPATKI NATIONAL MONUMENT
HOPI – NAVAJO LANDS SUNSET CRATER NATIONAL MONUMENT
LAKE POWELL AREA WALNUT CANYON NATIONAL MONUMENT
METEOR CRATER MONTEZUMA CASTLE NATIONAL MONUMENT

COVER: The Battleship at Dusk

WESTERN TRAILS PUBLICATIONS

GRAND CANYON
COUNTRY

Virginia Clark

WESTERN TRAILS PUBLICATIONS
P.O.Box 1697
San Luis Obispo, Ca., 93406

LEGENDS

BLACK

—— MAIN ROADS

· · · · SECONDARY ROADS

🚙 JEEP ROADS

👤 RANGER STATION

🔺 CAMPGROUND

🪑 PICNIC AREA

TOPOGRAPHICAL MAPS
½" denotes 1 mile

RED

· · · · · TRAILS

— · — PARK BOUNDARY LINE

- - - INDIAN RESERVATIONS
and NATIONAL FORESTS

TABLE OF

CONTENTS

THE GRAND CANYON

Connie Rudd

The wonder of this vast crack in the earth's surface is as awesome now as it was when the first white man discovered it long ago. Upon entering the Grand Canyon country through the forests of pine and juniper or fir and spruce, the initial view of this huge gaping crevice is absolutely breathtaking. To be suddenly facing the buttes and temples across the great abyss, one might question - How did this all come about?

The Grand Canyon is a great rugged gash cut by the Colorado River through the high Kaibab, Kanab, Uinkaret, and Shivwits Plateaus for some 277 miles, is over a mile deep, and varies in width from 600' to 17 miles. It is 5840' deep at the North Rim and 4500' on the South Rim with many side canyons of gullies, cliffs, buttes and temples. The aspects and magnitude of this spectacular, colorful display are difficult to fully grasp at one viewing.

Over 65 million years ago the earth's movement formed a domed tableland known as the Colorado Plateau. The uplift and tilting of the plateau raised the land many thousands of feet. Beginning high in the Rocky Mountains, the Colorado River casually flowed through the lands comprising of Arizona, Colorado and Utah to find its way eventually by gravity to the Gulf of California. As the river cut deeper and wider the waters became increasingly faster. The more resistant limestone and sandstone formed vertical cliffs as the softer, weaker materials were swept away.

While the river penetrated its course, gullies and canyons on either side were eroding from the annual melting snows and summer storms. Soft materials crumbled and the gravel, sand, silt, and sediments were washed to the sea. The remaining rock material, weakened by faulting at the time of the uplift and tilting of the plateau, formed the buttes, towers, temples, and sculptured rocks that stand vertically alone. The Colorado Plateau as a whole tips up to the south. Of the four 'subplateaus' the Grand Canyon is carved through, only the Kaibab Plateau is higher to the north. Thus, with the tilt of the Kaibab Plateau, the eating away was more pronounced and wider on the North side as runoffs from the waters flowed south down into the canyons and the Colorado River, while runoffs on the South side flowed south away from the canyons and River.

With the continuing erosive process scouring out gullies and crevices and widening the canyons bit by bit, the main body of water cut deeper and deeper taking the sediments to the sea. However, with the construction of the Hoover Dam, the Colorado River now empties into Lake Mead where the silt and sediments are settling. With the construction of the Glen Canyon Dam the waters are not as free-flowing as they once were, but are more regulated throughout the year, so it will be a long time before Lake Mead becomes a land mass.

Even though the Colorado River has a controlled flow which slows some of the action of the river, the rapids are not necessarily easier to float over or safer than when Major John Powell made his adventuresome trips down through the canyons. The debris that was once washed away by floods now remain in the River.

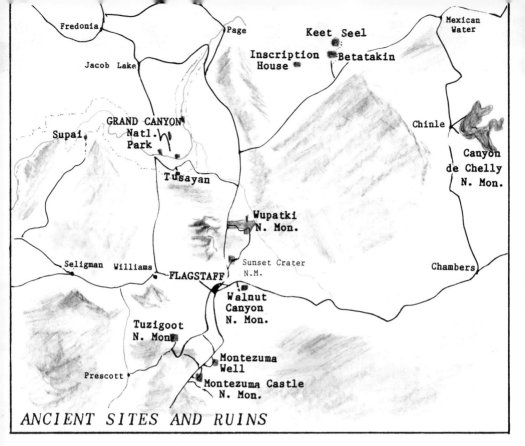

ANCIENT SITES AND RUINS

ANCIENT PEOPLE

In this ancient land, before the white man discovered the Grand Canyon country, ancient people lived who were called the Anasazi and Sinagua Indians. Throughout the Southwest ruins of pueblos with kivas, multi-storied cave and cliff dwellings with artifacts have been found and unearthed. They were the remains of an incredible number of prehistoric Indian communities that were found in steep canyons, high cliffs with overhanging ledges, and forested ridges. Wild game was plentiful as was the native plants that grew in meadows and along the streams, and sand bars and washes made irrigating the crops easy.

In the canyons and on the plateaus of the Colorado River environs settlements both large and small were abandoned in the twelfth to fourteenth centuries leaving the land to the lizards and mice. Historians and archaeologists have various theories as to their departure with indeterminate conclusions. However, it is known that at this time, historically, there was a widespread drought throughout the Southwest. With their existence depending on farming and hunting, they could not remain in an area where they could not sustain themselves.

The Anasazi Indians at Tusayan on the South Rim left their dwellings around 1150 AD, while at Betatakin and Keet Seel they left about 1300 AD. The Sinagua Indians at Walnut Canyon and Montezuma Castle abandoned their homes about 1250 AD.

Besides growing their own crops, these Indians used native plants for food, medicinal, and household purposes. The hardy yucca was a versatile plant as they made soup from the tender young blossoms; seeds were eaten raw or roasted; and the fruit was ground into flour and meal. A type of soap or 'amole' was made from the roots. The narrow, stiff spiny leaves were used for weaving baskets, mats, nets and sandals. Ropes made from fibrous leaves were used in the construction of ladders and in the tying of beams for their pueblos.

Sagebrush leaves were brewed into a medical tea, and the dead branches made a fragrant firewood. Protein and fat were obtained from pinyon pine nuts, which are very oily, and were boiled into gruel. Also, they shelled and dried the nuts for eating, which supplemented their diet. Pitch from the pinyons was used for waterproofing, chewing, and on their torches to light their rooms. Mormon tea, a long-jointed stem plant was popular as the stems were brewed for tea, and the seeds were ground for flour. Wild fruits and berries, in season, were gathered by the women and eaten. In the spring and early summer the young plants supplied them with ample greens.

With the 'atlatl', a simple spear thrower, they hunted the large game such as bighorn sheep, deer, and pronghorn antelope. Rabbits, hares, and squirrels could be killed by deftly throwing stones. They ate the meat and used the hides for clothing, blankets, door coverings, and ceremonial robes. From the bones and teeth they made their jewelry. With snares they caught the birds; the feathers decorated their clothes and ornaments in their religious rituals.

It was a communal life with the women sharing the responsibility for grinding the corn, preparing meals, and tending the children. They made baskets by plaiting, coiling, or twining fibers from wood, leaves and grasses. Baskets were used for cooking, carrying their babies, storing their food, and for all the necessities that had to be carried up and down the ladders. From the clay they found along the washes and banks of streams and rivers, they made beautiful pottery bowls and pitchers. The designs of slip or painted clay show much imagination and artistry.

The cliff dwellings built under the ledges were of rock piled on rocks cemented together with a muddy clay to form the rooms and partitions. In the more elaborate two, three, or five storied structures, as seen at Montezuma Castle, rough blocks of limestone were set in an earth mortar with ceilings of mud covered with timbers. Some ceiling beams were tied together with ropes and the floors above were packed with mud. In the Grand Canyon area the walls were stone with plaster and mud - mortar. Over the door they made smoke holes to ventilate the rooms.

Ladders were used to gain entrance to their homes built high up on the ledges and cliffs. Everything they needed, the water, food, firewood and materials gathered below in the canyons and washes, had to be brought up these ladders. When an enemy was sighted, they would take up the ladders and be safe in their impenetrable fortress. Note the long entrance ladder leading to the pueblo village at Keet Seel in the photograph.

Remnants of these ancient people's civilization can be found in many places on both the North and South Rims and in canyons along Garden, Clear, and Bright Angel Creeks, at Nankoweap Canyon and on Walhalla Plateau to name a few in Grand Canyon National Park. Other more extensive ruins can be seen in many areas of Arizona, New Mexico, southern Utah, and southwest Colorado.

Pueblos left by the Anasazi Indians are found at Tusayan on the South Rim of Grand Canyon National Park. Larger ancient villages can be visited at Keet Seel and Betatakin in Navajo National Monument. At Canyon de Chelly National Monument prehistoric Indian villages are at the base of the magnificent red cliffs and up in the ledges are cave dwellings. Today the Navajos live and farm in the lovely Chinle Valley. It is an important weaving area on the Navajo Reservation. Another large number of cliff dwellings that was a significant center of the Anasazi culture can be seen at Mesa Verde National Monument in southwest Colorado. Quite near by in southeastern Utah in the Hovenweep National Monument are ruins from both the Anasazi and Sinagua Indians. At Wupatki National Monument both groups of ancient people dwellings can be seen.

Ruins of the Sinagua Indian homes, broken pottery, baskets and other traces of their life can be viewed at Walnut Canyon Tuzigoot, and Montezuma Castle National Monuments.

Keet Seel

John K. Loleit

HISTORY AT A GLANCE

Prehistoric Indians inhabited the land, but it wasn't until 1540 that the first white men viewed the Grand Canyon and the Colorado River. Don Lopez de Cardenas with his party came upon it in their search for the fabled Seven Cities of Cibola.

1776 - Fathers Graces and Escalante visited the Havasupai Indians and noted the Canyon and River in their Journal.

1777 - Fathers Escalante and Dominquez crossed the Colorado, reaching the Hopi Indians at Old Ute Ford, now known as The Crossing of the Fathers.

1825 - James O. Pattie along with his father recorded a South Rim visit.

1858 - Lt. J.C. Ives made his initial account for the War Dept. and Dr. J.C. Newberry, geologist for the party wrote the first scientific report.
     - Jacob Hamlin, Mormon scout crossed the Colorado River at Old Ute Ford.

1864 - Hamlin crossed the River at where we call Lees Ferry.

1887 - James White claims the first solo trip down the River.

1869 - John Wesley Powell journeyed down the River making extensive geological surveys of terrain and canyons.

1870's The very remoteness of the Grand Canyon and Colorado River area became a refuge for fugitives and rustlers.

1871 - Meteor Crater was first discovered.

1872 - John D. Lee settled and established ferry service at the mouth of the Paria River, now Lees Ferry.

1883 - John Hance was the first settler on the South Rim.

1886 - Benjamin Harrison introduced a bill to make Grand Canyon a National Park.

1889 - Frank M. Brown drowned in the River while surveying for railroad possibilities.

1890 - Robert B. Stanton completed a railway survey of the River all the way to Gulf of Mexico.
     - William W. Bass established a tourist camp, and built a trans-canyon trail and cableway across the River.

1891 - Bright Angel Trail was improved from the original Indian trail.

1893 - Benjamin Harrison created Grand Canyon Forest Reserve.

1901 - First passenger train reached Grand Canyon on Sante Fe Railroad from Williams.

1902 - Francois Matthes, mapped Grand Canyon, and North Kaibab Trail improved. The first motor cars invaded the area.

1905 - El Tovar Hotel was built.

1906 - Montezuma Castle National Monument was established.

1908 - Grand Canyon National Monument was established.
     - Kolb brothers discovered Cheyava Falls.

1909 - Cummins-Douglas discovered Rainbow Bridge.

1910 - Rainbow Bridge National Monument established preserving the natural span.

1911 - Emery and Ellsworth Kolb and James Fagen went down the Colorado River from Green River to the Bright Angel Trail and took the first motion pictures of the run.
     - Sante Fe Railroad constructed Hermit Trail.

Bright Angel Lodge, 1935   *N.P.S.Photo*

1912 - Charles Spenser steamboated from Warm Springs down to Lees Ferry.
1915 - Walnut Canyon National Monument was established to protect the ancient Indian dwellings.
1919 - Grand Canyon National Park was established.
1921 - The Fred Harvey Co. re-developed Rust Camp (1903) into Phantom Ranch.
1923 - USGS and Emery C. Dolb surveyed for possible dam sites.
1924 - Wupatki National Monument established to preserve ruins.
1928 - Kaibab Trail completed - first cross-canyon trail.
     - Kaibab Suspension Bridge built.
     - National Park Service administers control over the Bright Angel Trail.
1929 - Navajo Bridge built to replace Lees Ferry crossing.
1930 - Sunset Crater National Monument created to protect the cinder cone environment.
1932 - Grand Canyon National Monument established.
1933 - Desert View Watchtower was built by the Fred Harvey Co. and Santa Fe Railroad.
     - Pumping station at Roaring Springs built to supply water to both the North and South Rims.
1935 - Hoover Dam was completed, creating Lake Mead.
1936 - The River Trail was built by the CCC.
1937 - Haldane Holmstrom went from Green River down to Hoover Dam alone.
1938 - Walnut Canyon National Monument enlarged to present size.
     - First inflatable boat was floated down the River.
1939 - Tuzigoot National Monument was established to protect the prehistoric Indian ruins.
1947 - Montezuma Well was added to Monument Castle National Monument.
1949 - First powerboat journeyed down through the canyon from Lees Ferry to Lake Mead.
1950 - George White pioneered the large river raft trips.
1957 - Page was founded for the Glen Canyon Dam workers.
1960 - First jet boats went through Canyon from Lake Mead up to Lava Falls.
1964 - Glen Canyon Dam completed, creating Lake Powell.
1970's Guided river raft tours through the Grand Canyon and
to   Mule Rides down the Canyon become popular.
1980's   *15*

Park Headquarters, 1920's   *N.P.S. Photo*

GRAND CANYON VILLAGE

There are many services and accommodations in Grand Canyon Village to meet the many needs of the thousands of visitors who come from many lands to see the wonders of this park. There are two magnificent old lodges with historic background. In 1905 El Tovar Hotel was built and in 1935 the Bright Angel Lodge was constructed after the Santa Fe Railroad came into Grand Canyon.

Modern lodges and motels, some quite luxurious, offer forest and canyon views with up-to-date conveniences that include gift shops, restaurants, cafeterias, and cocktail lounges. Advanced reservations are necessary from May to October. There is also an International Youth Hostel located on Tonto Street near the Ranger Office. Some facilities are open all year.

In the Village are numerous curio and gift shops including Indian stores and museums such as the Hopi House, a representation of an Indian pueblo. It has a leather-strap door handle, and displays of the Hopi Indian basketry, pottery, and weaving with old antique furniture.

To supply necessities and comfort to the traveler there is a beauty and barber shop, bank, laundromat, pharmacy and medical clinic, newsstand, pet kennel, propane, post office, automobile service stations, service clubs such as the Rotary and Lions Clubs, showers, sporting goods stores with rentals of the necessary backpacking equipment, supermarket and delicatessan, taxi, telephones, and telegraph service. Some of these are not operating during the winter season.

There is a campground located in the Village and at Desert View, a trailer park with full hook-ups among the pines, a dump station, and several picnic areas. Ticketron handles the Mather Campground reservations for May to September only. The open and clean campgrounds are attractively separated with many pull-through sites among the pines and junipers. Tables and grills are provided. An area for group camping is also available.

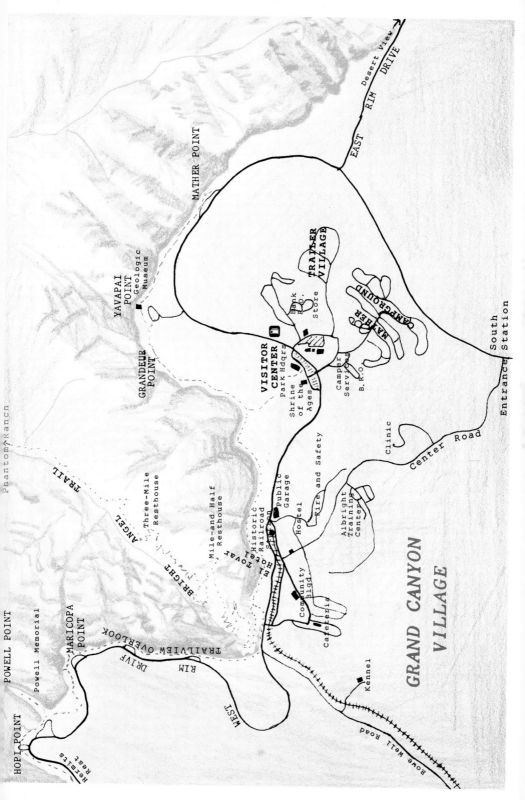

GRAND CANYON VILLAGE

HOPI POINT

POWELL POINT

Powell Memorial

MARICOPA POINT

Hermits Rest

TRAILVIEW OVERLOOK

WEST RIM DRIVE

BRIGHT ANGEL TRAIL

Phantom Ranch

GRANDEUR POINT

YAVAPAI POINT

Geologic Museum

MATHER POINT

Three-Mile Resthouse

Mile-and Half Resthouse

Historic Railroad

El Tovar Hotel

Public Garage

Hostel

Fire and Safety

Community Bldg.

Cafeteria

Albright Training Center

Kennel

VISITOR CENTER

Park Hdqrs

Shrine of the Ages

Store

Bank P.O.

Camper Services

B.R.O.

TRAILER VILLAGE

MATHER CAMPGROUND

Clinic

Center Road

South Entrance Station

Rowe Well Road

EAST RIM DRIVE

Desert View

17

West From South Rim   *Dean Clark*

VISTOR CENTER

The Visitor Center offers exhibits, an Information Desk, postings of bulletins for daily and weekly schedules of walks, talks, weather, and road conditions. Slide orientation programs are held at the Center.

For sale are books and pamphlets in several languages for adults and children as well as geological charts and topographical maps. On display are interesting historical artifacts from early expeditions and dioramas of the early explorers and other geological aspects of the land.

The Ranger Naturalists conduct walks at the Village, Tusayan Ruins and Desert View during the summer months. The evening talks are held at the Mather Amphitheater and at the Sage Loop Campfire Circle during the summer. In the winter they are held at the Shrine of the Ages Auditorium. Permits to hike down into the Inner Canyon via all trails are obtained at the Backcountry Reservation Office in the Camper Service Loop.

The Grand Canyon Natural History Association publishes the Grand Canyon Guides that give current pertinent information and scheduled activities. They also publish worthwhile books, self-guiding brochures and pamphlets on the many phases of life in and around the Park.

At Yavapai Museum there are short geology talks throughout the day. In the Geology Museum are rock specimens, geology time clock, charts, maps, and large observation windows offering excellent canyon views. Public restrooms are situated here.

Out at Yavapai Point there is a good view of the O'Neill Butte and Cedar Ridge to the east. A short walk to the west is Grandeur Point with another good view to the west and north.

SOUTH RIM NATURE TRAIL

This trail extends along the rim edge affording extensive vistas of the changing coloration of the canyons and cliffs beyond. The perimeter journey leads from Hermits Rest, at times paralleling the West Rim Drive eastward to the Yavapai Museum and Mather Point beyond the Visitor Center. A beginning or ending of any trip can be made at any point. This trail is ideal for a rewarding early morning promenade, or an evening stroll to watch the sun lowering beyond the western horizon, or a leisurely walk to acclimate with the some 7000' elevation before venturing down into the Inner Canyon. Check at the Visitor Center for sunrise and sunset hours.

The trail is paved west as far as Maricopa Point and east to Yavapai Museum. It is well-graded and level part of the way but very steep from the West Rim intersection to Trailview 1. The trail west of Maricopa Point is very rough. Sometimes it is necessary to walk beside the road.

There is a self-guiding nature pamphlet available explaining the ecological and geological aspects of the 1.5 mile section from El Tovar Hotel to the Visitor Center and beyond to Yavapai Museum. Ranger-guided walks acquaint the visitor with the finer points of canyon history, geology, flora and fauna. Check for time and location of the various walks within the Village area at the Visitor Center.

Watching the ravens, swifts, and swallows soaring in the canyon uplifts or observing the pinyon-juniper forest community are worthy facets of this nature trail. The picturesque, twisted, shaggy-barked juniper trees and stumps which shelter the yucca plants and grasses beneath, and the mistletoe living off the junipers and pinyon pines are unique. The shrubs blooming in their season, and the squirrels foraging among the ponderosa cones add their beauty to this magnificent setting.

Juniper on South Rim Nature Trail   *Connie Rudd*

19

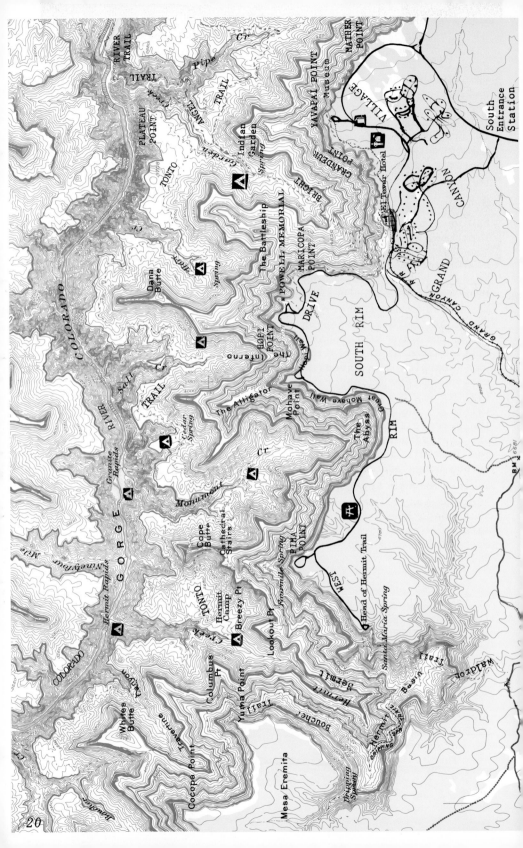

Looking up Bright Angel Canyon   *Dean Clark*

WEST RIM DRIVE

Paralleling the rim of the canyon, the West Rim Drive has many lookout points along the 8.0-mile road from Bright Angel Lodge to Hermits Rest. At Trailview, the first overlook, the El Tovar stands out above the green forest across the side canyon and hikers along the Bright Angel Trail can be spotted. Plateau Point can be seen below. Maricopa Point offers an excellent view of the Battleship, west of Garden Creek. Powell Point displays a memorial to Major John Wesley Powell. He led the 1869 expedition with ten brave men to run the turbulant and dangerous rapids down the Colorado River.

At Hopi, Mohave, and Pima Points the Park Rangers give interpretative information on the surrounding country during the summer months. From these vista points the Colorado River can be seen far below. Hopi Point, which juts out further north than the others, is an excellent area to watch the sunset. For safety in precipitous places, railings are provided. Care must be taken when wandering or picture-taking along the edge and on the rocks as loose gravel can be dangerous.

These overlooks afford unsurpassed views of the many temples, buttes, and geological formations of the Inner Canyon and of the North Rim country. Watch the color and lighting change with the change of time and weather. In the early morning the eastern sunlight upon the rocks deep in the canyon makes the lines of the cliffs sharp. Later in the day, as the sun travels across the sky, these cliffs become long, dark shadows with intensive color.

Hermits Rest has a snack bar, curio shop, and comfort station. Many years ago the Fred Harvey Company built this unique cave-like structure with its large windows to enable visitors to fully enjoy the spectacular views across the canyon, down to the Colorado River and beyond.

There are guided bus tours with comfortable motor coach travel that stops at the various viewpoint along the drive. These tours leave from the Bright Angel Lodge.

RESERVATIONS AND TOURS

The Bright Angel, Yavapai, and Maswick Lodges have Transportation Desks that handles reservations and arrangements for various in-park and out-park bus and air tours. Bus tours in modern motor coaches within the Park go to Desert View and Hermits Rest. There is a special Sunset Tour every evening during the summer only. Transportation Desks arrange for daily buses from Williams and Flagstaff which connect with the other major commercial bus and airlines. The Bright Angel Lodge Transportation Desk handles the reservations for the one or two-day mule trips that go down to Plateau Point or Phantom Ranch.

MULE TOURS TO INNER CANYON

The one-day tour follows down the Bright Angel Trail, and after a rest stop at Indian Garden, goes out to Plateau Point. The tour returns up the trail after spending some time enjoying the awesome view down into the Colorado River.

The two-day tour also follows down the Bright Angel Trail and after the rest stop at Indian Garden proceeds down Garden Creek. At the Colorado River the River Trail goes eastward to the tunnel before crossing the Kaibab Suspension Bridge. From there the trail follows along the north shore of the River and up Bright Angel Canyon to Phantom Ranch for the overnight stay.

Sitting under the cottonwood trees refreshes the spirits after the arduous trip down the canyon. The next day the ascent is made up the shorter, although steeper South Kaibab Trail, returning to the Bright Angel Lodge in the mid-afternoon.

Mule trips are offered at the North Rim to October 15th. There are half-day and full-day tours down into the canyon. The horseback riding trips along the Rim are available on an hourly or daily basis. Contact the Grand Canyon Trail Rides Desk in the lobby of the Grand Canyon Lodge for more information.

PHANTOM RANCH

This sub-tropical oasis located within the Inner Canyon is reached by the Bright Angel, the South Kaibab, and the North Kaibab Trails. Operated by the Fred Harvey Company on the American Plan, the Ranch offers good meals and comfortable beds. They serve a Hikers Special Dinner and some family-style meals, a hearty breakfast, and they make up sack lunches. Campers at the Bright Angel Campground may reserve meals. They also have beer and drinks for sale.

The stone-cornered cottages sleep up to four, or ten bunkbeds for groups. The dorms are separated as to sex and have ten beds each. Both are air-cooled in the summer when the temperatures get above 100°, and are heated in the winter. All of the beds are made up with sheets, blankets, and pillows. They provide towels and soap for showers, which are located in the central building with the dorms.

All reservations must be confirmed before beginning the trip down to the Ranch. Cancelled reservations are then resold at 9 AM each day at the Bright Angel Transportation Deak at the Lodge on the South Rim.

MULE RIDE SAFETY

Certain safety measures are taken for the mule tours to secure the visitor's comfort as well as for the well-being of the mules. It is a vigorous trip and precautions must be met.

All tours start at Bright Angel Lodge where the rider is weighed. The maximum weight, with no exceptions, is 200 pounds fully dressed. To really enjoy the Inner Canyon experience, it is necessary to be in good physical condition as sufficient strength is needed to guide the mules at turns and junctions. No pregnant women are allowed, and participants must be 4'7" tall. A thorough knowledge of English is needed to understand the guide.

The guides are in charge and their instructions must be followed. The trails are steep and those afraid of heights should not attempt the trip. The Bright Angel Trail goes down a side canyon in a valley while the South Kaibab Trail follows along the ridge. It is not necessary to know how to ride, but it certainly helps.

Wearing apparel consists of long pants, a big brimmed hat that ties under the chin so that it doesn't fly off to hold up the party to retrieve it, or to scare the mules. Good walking shoes, not sandals or the open-toed kind, are necessary for the most comfortable riding and walking. Personal gear is put into duffle bags and packed on the mule's back. Only essential items should be taken. It is a strenuous, yet exhilerating trip and well worth the momentary agony of saddle sores or stiff limbs.

Mule Ride on Bright Angel Trail   *Connie Rudd*

OTHER SERVICES

Religious services include an Interdenominational Community Church with Youth Sunday School and Midweek Bible Study; El Cristo Rey Catholic Church; Grand Canyon Baptist Church with Midweek Bible Study held at the Shrine of the Ages; Grand Canyon Assembly of God with Sunday and Midweek Worship Services at the Shrine of the Ages; and the Church of Jesus Christ of Latter-Day Saints with meetings also held at the Shrine of the Ages.

The National Park Service provides free wheelchairs for use in the Park. They have publications in Braille, on tape, or in large print. Check at the Visitor Center or Yavapai Museum for further details on specific information for the physically handicapped, including the use of wheelchair lifts and shuttle buses.

To eliminate tourist frustrations, confusion and pollution of the Park during the heavily visited summer months - Memorial Day to Labor Day - free shuttle buses are available in the Village with stops conveniently located to cover the most trafficked areas. Buses go as far as Hermits Rest on the West Rim Drive with frequent stops at key points along the way. The West Rim Drive shuttle begins just west of Bright Angel Lodge. There are no automobiles allowed west of this point during the summer when the West Rim Drive shuttle buses are in operation.

SOUTH OF PARK

South beyond the entrance to the Park, many tourist services and accommodations are available that allow visitation into the Park. At Park Boundary there are several lodges and service stations.

Seven miles south of the Visitor Center TUSAYAN (Hwy.64), has a full range of tourist facilities that include a Tourist Center, lodging, restaurants, service stations with diesel fuel and propane, markets, post office, telephones, car rentals, a Camper Village, IMAX Theatre, horseback riding, curio and gift shops, and a Heliport where various tours originate.

South of Tusayan at the Grand Canyon Airport, tour flights of different distances with a variety of prices and durations take off. Beside the over-canyon flights, they offer trans-canyon travel from the South Rim to the North Rim. Other tours go to Havasupai Indian Reservation, Monument Valley, Lake Powell, and the Painted Desert. In the Grand Canyon Airline Terminal historic documents and photographs are on display.

Just past the airstrip is the Forest Service campground - Tent X (6600'), open from May to October with picnicking, camping for tents and trailers with handicap facilities. There is drinking water and pit toilets.

South of Tent X Campground, a road leads east to RED BUTTE which has a Lookout Tower to view the San Francisco Peaks and the Colorado Plateau.

Dean Clark

Looking Eastward   *Lewis Clark*

EAST RIM DRIVE

The 23.0 mile drive eastward to Desert View from the Grand Canyon Village continues through the pinyon-juniper forest. It is, however, more open with sage and Gambel oaks. Trees are not as large and further apart.

The first major turnout is at Yaki Point. Looking down into the canyon are rewarding views of Plateau Point, the Tonto Platform, and O'Neill Butte. The South Kaibab Trailhead and Parking area is reached by this road. Portable restrooms, but no water, and telephones are available.

Grandview Point is the trailhead for the Grandview Trail to the Horseshoe Mesa and Tonto Trail. It is advisable to wear good hiking shoes and be prepared for sudden thunderstorms when traveling on the trails into the Inner Canyon. The outstanding views at this Point are of the canyon and trail below and east to Hance Creek.

There are several picnic sites and many turnouts along the road between Yaki Point and Desert View. Just past the picnic area at Buggeln Hill is a pull-out to view the formation known as the Sinking Ship.

At Moran Point above Hance Canyon the Coronado Butte can be seen. It was named for the early explorer who led his expedition into this country to search for the fabled Seven Golden Cities of Cibola.

The Tusayan Ruins and Museum, reached by a short spur to the south, depict the life of the early Southwest Indians who lived here in the twelfth century before the white man came. They are believed to be the forefathers of the modern Hopi Indians. In the museum there are displays of their lifestyle, culture and crafts. A self-guiding tour around the ancient ruins shows the kiva, their living and storage quarters. A brochure describes how they hunted and struggled to live in a land with little water and poor soil conditions.

Lipan Point is the trailhead and parking area for the Tanner Trail. Here are some of the finest views of the Colorado River and of the San Francisco Mountain raising 12,633' on the southern horizon.

DESERT VIEW

Watchtower   *Lewis Clark*

Desert View is the eastern Visitor Center with a seasonal campground, picnic area, service station, restaurant, general store, fountain, gift shops, and the well-known 70' high Watchtower. The Ranger Station supplies information and assistance. The Ranger Naturalist programs include campfire talks, sunset walks, and geology talks at the Watchtower.

The Watchtower was built on the brink of the Rim in 1933 by the Fred Harvey Company and the Santa Fe Railroad as an observation station and rest stop for their visitors. At the base of the tower is a reproduction of an Indian kiva, which is a sacred ceremonial chamber of the pueblo Indians. On the walls and ceilings are decorated symbols and pictographs of ceremonial paintings and legends.

The raven's-eye view from the top of the Watchtower is an unusual and tremendous one. Far to the north is the Kaibab National Forest, across to the east is the Painted Desert and the Navajo Indian Reservation, below is the mighty Colorado River with the Tanner Trail and Rapids, and south is the San Francisco Peaks. Strong binoculars offer closer views for all these points. At the Watchtower the ancient people and the ancient land are seen in all their magnificence.

From Desert View to Cameron the road drops down through the Upper Basin Rim or Coconino Rim, past the Little Colorado River Gorge to junction with Hwy.89. In the Navajo Reservation the Indians sell their jewelry and souvenirs in parking areas off the road. Excellent views of the Little Colorado River and Gorge can be seen.

Little Colorado River Gorge   *Dean Clark*

CAMERON

At Cameron, on Hwy.89 leading north from Flagstaff are the motels, service stations, restaurants, gift and curio shops, a campground, and trailer parks. Some services are open only in the summer season from Memorial Day to Labor Day.

Once officially known as Tanner's Crossing, Cameron is situated on the banks of the Little Colorado River. Ralph Cameron, a U.S. Senator was one of Arizona's early pioneers who developed some of the first trails down into the canyons from the old Indian footpaths. He was one of the first to develop tourism within the Park. He also had a copper mining operation.

The highway bridge now traverses the Little Colorado River where early pioneers crossed as they followed the old Mormon Trail. The trail extended from Utah to settlements in Arizona and New Mexico. At this place in the river, the bottom was free of quicksand and the firm rock base enabled the wagons to make a less hazardous trip across. Seth B. Tanner, a Mormon pioneer, assisted these pioneers and the crossing was named in his honor.

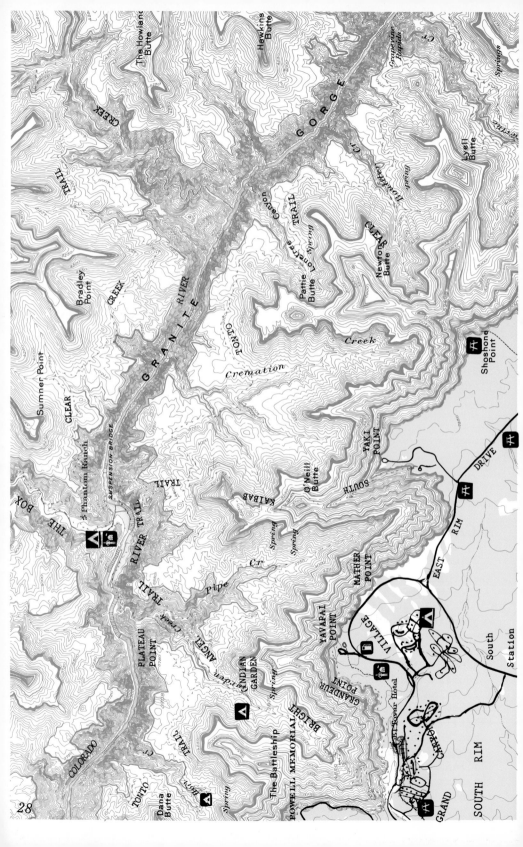

TRAILS TO INNER CANYON

Backpacking on the trails of Grand Canyon to reach the Inner Canyon and the Colorado River is just the opposite from the usual mountain experience. The descent is at the cool of the morning while the sun is behind and the ascent up the steep trails is later in the hotter part of the day. Those last few miles are the most difficult. It is necessary to be in top physical condition as the trails are generally rocky and hard in some sections. Remember the lower the trail into the Inner Canyon the hotter it becomes.

Carrying water is essential (at least a quart per person). The heat of the day, the temperatures from the cliffs, the dust from the trail, and the dryness of the desert atmosphere makes the hiker very thirsty.

The growth of environmental awareness during the past decade has aided in minimizing adverse impacts and maximizing the recreational usage. Wilderness Permits are necessary for overnight hiking only. Day travel does not require one. When making reservations for any proposed trip. be sure to include dates, the number of people in the party, the specific camp area desired, and length of stay. Hikers arriving without reservations may be able to obtain a cancelled one at the Backcountry Reservation Office on the South Rim to be put on the daily waiting list.

At a great deal of expense and effort switchbacks were built to ease the pain of going down steep terrain and hiking up the canyons. Therefore, it is mandatory not to cross-cut any switchback or break down the trails.

Nothing should be left behind including cigarette butts. What is packed in must be packed out. All human waste must be buried and the wet toilet tissue must be brought back out in plastic bags.

No fires are allowed in the canyon. There are many foods readily available in markets that need no cooking. If cooking is necessary, a backpack stove or sterno is recommended.

No matter how tempting it is to swim in the cold, turbulent Colorado River, it is prohibited as well as dangerous.

The best common-sense advice to enjoy the Inner Canyon is to prepare well for the trip. Think of what you are doing while on the trail and how it might affect others who follow. They would like to find the backcountry in the same condition as you would – unspoiled. That way, everyone can obtain the ultimate wilderness experience.

Trails are in use areas or Management Zones. The Corridor is for the popular Bright Angel, South Kaibab and North Kaibab Trails. The Threshold Zone has designated camp sites, but the trails are unmaintained as in the Primitive Zone with camping at-large. The Undeveloped Zone speaks for itself.

REMEMBER: No feeding of animals. No pets below the Rims. No firearms, motorized vehicles or bicycles on the trails. No rock throwing into the canyons. No molesting or collecting of flora, fauna or artifacts.

River Trail, Suspension Bridge, and Phantom Ranch   *Connie Rudd*

BRIGHT ANGEL TRAIL

Descending along the footpath of ancient Indians to the depth of the Colorado River below, the Bright Angel trail passes beside the strated walls of ancient earth formations. A geological breakthrough of the Bright Angel Fault provided this natural route down into the canyon. At Indian Garden the pure springs with its water supply help make the canyon journey more enjoyable. Much of the trail can be seen from the overlooks on the South Rim as it leads down to the River. There is an ever-changing display of wildlife and environment as the trail goes deeper into the canyon.

Early mining prospectors were the first white men to use the initial primitive trail made by the Indians. As operations in the mines developed, it became necessary to construct a more substantial trail. The political and private interests of this trail within Grand Canyon National Park was a problem. For some time the trail belonged to the Coconino County and a toll was charged for its use. In 1928 the National Park Service assumed complete control.

The trail is well-marked, well maintained, and well traveled. Daily mule train tours use this trail to go down and out to Plateau Point and return. The two-day mule tours use this trail to descend to Phantom Ranch. It should be remembered when meeting a mule train to stand quietly on one side of the trail until the entire train has completely passed.

There are two tunnels within the first mile before the first group of switchbacks. At Milepost 1.5 and 3.0 there are resthouses and emergency telephones. Water is available during the summer months. After the 2.0 mile corner, pictographs made by prehistoric Indians of animals and birds can be seen under a large boulder of the Supai formation.

The Havasupai Tribe, the forefathers of the Indians living in Havasu Canyon today, once inhabited Indian Garden growing corn, beans, and squash. Now situated under the cottonwoods is a free, designated campground. This cool oasis for hikers and mule tour riders offers picnic tables, purified water, sanitary facilities, emergency telephone, and a Ranger on duty. Fifteen sites are for individuals and a separate site for groups up to sixteen persons can be reserved. Due to the extensive usage of the Indian Garden area, the limit per hiker is for two nights per site, per hike. No supplies can be obtained here.

From Indian Garden the Tonto-Plateau Point Trails goes north and west through a desert environment with plants and animals adapting to the arid conditions. Most animals may not be observed as they are more active in the cool of night rather than forging during the heat of the day. At Plateau Point the spectacular panorama includes the Colorado River with several series of rapids, and the numerous temples and buttes on the skyline.

Beyond Indian Garden and the Tonto-Plateau turnoff are two routes to the two suspension bridges that span the River. The Bright Angel Trail follows along Garden Creek through the Tapeats Narrows after the junction of the Tonto Trail leading east to meet the South Kaibab Trail.

At one time the Anasazi Indians lived in the Tapeats cliffs growing squash, beans, and corn as water was abundant. From the yucca plant they obtained food and fibers for baskets, ropes, and sandals. They hunted deer, bighorn sheep, and small animals found in this Life Zone. The creek is contaminated now and should not be used for drinking.

The trail veers eastward before descending the switchbacks called the Devils Corkscrew. They were blasted out of the sheer cliffs of the Vishnu Group for some 500 feet. The trail then follows along the creek to meet the River Trail. This water is not safe to drink either.

RIVER TRAIL

This trail, as the name suggests, follows for 1.7 miles along the bottom of the canyon above the muddy, roaring, mighty Colorado River to the silver suspension footbridge. This trail was blasted out from the solid rock of the Vishnu Group of the Precambrian geological era in 1936 by the Civilian Conservation Corps. The River Resthouse at the Pipe Creek junction, has an emergency telephone.

This footbridge is also used to hold the water pipeline that extends from Roaring Springs, north up in the Bright Angel Canyon. to Indian Garden. From there the water is pumped up to the South Rim.

Along South Kaibab Trail   *Connie Rudd*

SOUTH
KAIBAB
TRAIL

This steep, rugged 6.3 miles trail leading from Yaki Point down to the Colorado River crossing, where it meets the North Kaibab Trail, should be traveled more in the spring and autumn than in the hot summer months. There is no respite from the sun beating down. With no water available along the trail, or shade in rest areas, or campgrounds to the bottom of the canyon, it can be an arduous experience. It is a common practice for backpackers to descend on the South Kaibab Trail and ascend via the Bright Angel Trail where water and shaded rest can be obtained. The guided mule trips return to the top of the rim on the South Kaibab Trail as it is shorter than the Bright Angel Trail.

This is a well-built, well marked trail. It was constructed during the time of the political hassle over the ownership of the Bright Angel Trail. Most of the way lies along the prominent ridges offering outstanding and extensive vistas of the canyons and cliffs. It is an incredible display of the buttes, towers, and escarpments of red and buff mixed with the grayish-green shrubs where brilliant sunlight and dark shadows enhance the rock fortresses.

Along the trail are geological interpretative signs. There is a self-guiding informative pamphlet available on fossils and other phenomena. The descent is made through the formation of the earth, as seen by the varying rock strata - from fossilization in the Kaibab Limestone layer through the sandstone and shale of the Supai formation, past the Redwall Limestone down to the Vishnu Group.

At Cedar Ridge, a mile-and-a-half from the trailhead, is a picnic area with the O'Neill Butte standing in full view.A fossil fern exhibit is placed here. For a short, not too strenuous walk through the centuries of the earth's forming, a hike down to Cedar Ridge and return can be a good, vigorous one-day trip. Allow some resting time to fully enjoy the magnificence and the beauty of this Inner Canyon. It is an excellent trip for beginners or for those wishing an easy walk less than three miles. No permits are required for the day hike. Toilet facilities are provided.

South Kaibab Trail from Yaki Point   *MAC*

After Cedar Ridge the trail proceeds north down around the
O'Neill Butte, switchbacks down and around the Natural Arch to
enter the Tonto Platform. The trail then junctions with the
Tonto Trail which goes eastward along the bench above the river
to connect with the Grandview Trail. At the Tipoff the Tonto
Trail follows westward for some 4.3 miles to Indian Garden on
the Bright Angel Trail. There is an emergency telephone and
toilet facilities at the Tipoff.

Continuing on the South Kaibab Trail, the switchbacks lead
down through the Inner Gorge to the Colorado River via the 100'
tunnel. The tunnel was carved out of the solid granite Vishnu
Group rock to reach the Kaibab Suspension Foot and Mule Bridge.
It is some 65' above the water and 450' long. Mule trains use
this bridge as the floor is covered so as not to spook the
mules when crossing, as they cannot see the river.

The North Kaibab Trail then follows along the north shore
and up to the Phantom Ranch, Ranger Station and Bright Angel
Campground. For an overnight trip, accommodations are available
at the Ranch. For those camping, the campground has 33 sites
for individuals and two sites for groups. Reservations are required for both the Ranch and the campground. The Kaibab Trail
is the only cross-canyon joining of the North and South Rims.

Hermits Rest   *Dean Clark*

HERMIT TRAIL

In the early 1900's the Santa Fe Railway Company built and maintained the Hermit Trail to reach the Hermit Camp. Evidences of this camp can be seen along the trail today. The Fred Harvey Company offered accommodations and a wilderness experience unsurpassed to these early visitors. This was a popular entry into the Inner Canyon during the time the Bright Angel Trail was a tollroad and not under the jurisdiction of the National Park Service.

From Hermits Rest the trail descends the Coconino formation south to junction with the Waldron Trail coming down north from Horsethief Tank. (Reached by the fire/jeep road west of the Bright Angel Wash.)

After the Santa Maria Springs the trail passes through the Redwall Limestone formation via a series of switchbacks called the Cathedral Stairs. Circling around south of Cope Butte the trail enters the Tonto Platform to meet the Tonto Trail. This is an unmaintained trail with washouts and recommended for the EXPERIENCED CANYON TRAVELER ONLY. Water at Santa Maria Springs needs to be purified.

There are two designated camping sites - Hermit Creek and down by Hermit Rapids. See map page 20.

The BOUCHER TRAIL begins at Hermits Rest and branches to the north from Dipping Springs Trail. It was named after Louis Boucher who was an old hermit living in the Dipping Springs area for many years. The trail is unmaintained and should be traveled by EXPERIENCED BACKPACKERS ONLY. Going north to Yuma Point, the trail enters the headwaters of Travertine Canyon, proceeds over the saddle to the east branch of Boucher Creek, then past White Butte to meet the Tonto Trail.

The DIPPING SPRINGS TRAIL crosses the head of Hermit Creek Canyon for a mile and a half to meet the Hermit Trail. A jeep/fire road leads from the south of the Park to Dipping Spring.

TONTO TRAIL

This 72-mile trail along the Tonto Platform extends from Red Canyon on the east to Garnet Creek on the west above the Granite Gorge of the Colorado River. It follows through an arid desert environment. It is seldom hiked continuously at one time but rather used as a connecting route or for loop trips. In the western section, locating the trail at washouts is necessary. Usually there is little traffic west of Travertine Canyon, with the exception of the South Bass Canyon area.

There are designated campsites west of Garden Creek and at Indian Garden. See the map on page 20.

The hot, dry desert provides no trees for shade and little water. The Tonto Platform lies between the redwall river cliffs and the ponderosa-pinyon-juniper forest on the rim. All living creatures and plants have learned to exist in their own unique, exceptional way.

The pocket mouse and kangaroo rat manufacture their bodily moisture needs from the dry foods they eat. Some desert animals have a light color to absorb less sun rays or to be camouflaged from predators. Other animals burrow deep under prickly bushes during the day and forage only at night. The jackrabbit has a special built-in air conditioner with his long ears.

Flowers and shrubs have learned to survive in the burning heat and dryness in strange and varied ways. Some plants have a few leaves at the base of their stem or small leaves such as the Mormon tea. Other plants shed their leaves altogether in the summer or have fuzzy coverings. The desert holly has shiny leaves to detract the hot sun rays. The creasote bush has waxy leaves and spread their roots to capture as much mositure as possible. The cacti family have adapted by storing water in their stem pads.

From the Tonto Platform the impressive and colorful rock towers, buttes, and escarpments stand out on the skyline. The wall of the Inner Gorge and the mighty, murky Colorado River are not far below.

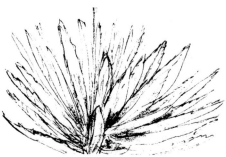

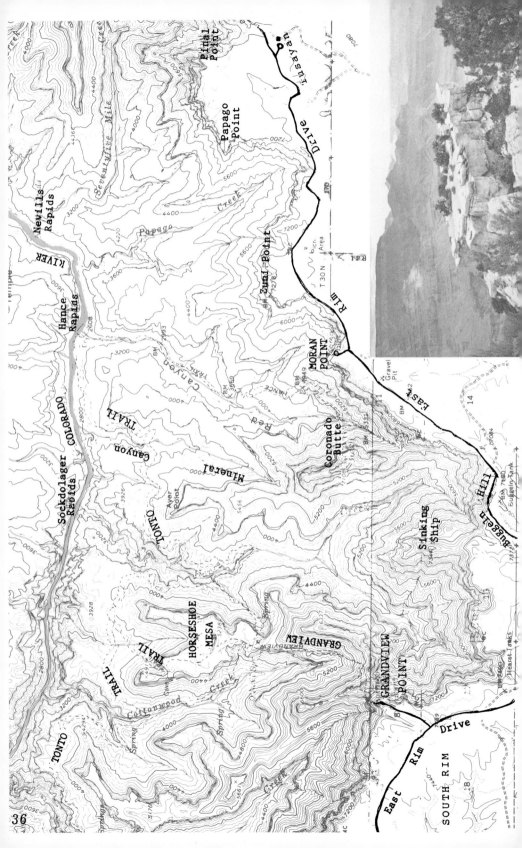

36

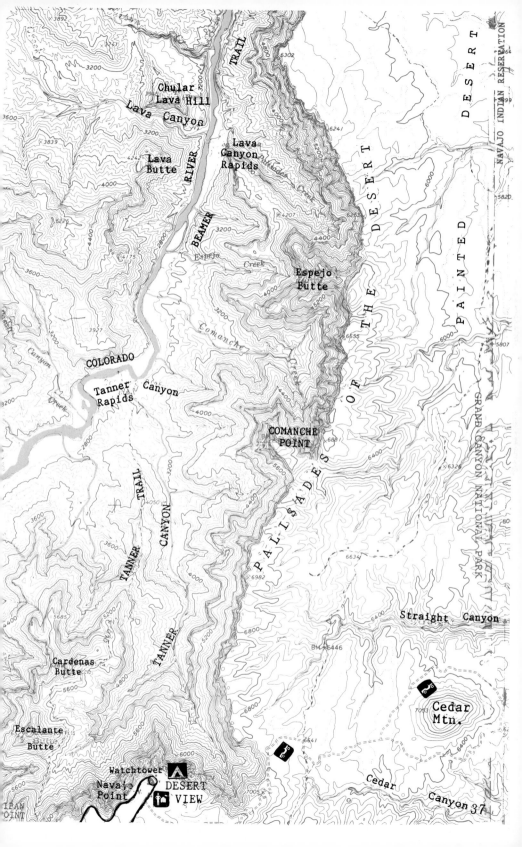

GRANDVIEW TRAIL

This old trail leading down to the Horseshoe Mesa area and to junction with the west-east Tonto Trail was built in the late 1800's. Copper claims on Horseshoe Mesa and other sites in the Grand Canyon area necessitated the upgrading of the old Indian footpaths.

Leaving the South Rim at Grandview Point (7400') the trail follows north through a steep, rough descent of the Coconino Sandstone formation, then extends downward more gradually to the Mesa. There are numerous loop trip possibilities between Cottonwood Creek and the Tonto Trail.

The Grandview Trail is not maintained or as well traveled as the more popular Bright Angel or South Kaibab Trails. IT IS RECOMMENDED FOR THE EXPERIENCED CANYON BACKPACKER ONLY as there are some washout, although locating the trail is not difficult. It is in a Threshold Management Zone. This means it is an area with some facilities and some development but not as much as in the more populated Corridor Zone. Some sections of the trail are narrow with loose gravelly rocks and sand so care should be taken.

There is no water along the trail but on the west fork up from Cottonwood Creek are some springs. The O'Neill Spring is not reliable. There is a designated campground on top of the Redwall Limestone formation at the south end of Horseshoe Mesa. There are Indian ruins to explore, scattered mining artifacts, and an old mine shaft. This should be entered carefully. The cave on the western section of the Mesa is assessable.

The RED CANYON – NEW HANCE TRAIL is not maintained and is listed under the Primitive Management Zone with no facilities or designated camping sites. Camping is at-large. This trail is recommended for ONLY THE HARDY, WELL-EXPERIENCED DESERT BACK-PACKER. There are some very dangerous, precipitous areas with many washouts.

Grandview Trail Country   MAC

Up The Colorado River Along the Beamer Trail   Dean Clark

TANNER TRAIL

Once referred to as the "Horsethief Trail", the Tanner Trail was one of the five built to reach the copper mines along the Colorado River. The trailhead parking is at Lipan Point.

This 9.0 mile trail is not maintained. It is narrow and at times difficult to traverse and DEFINITELY NOT FOR BEGINNERS. The trail is exposed and hot with no respite with shade. Only the experienced desert and backcountry hiker can be able to withstand the rough conditions.

The trail descends on the west arm of the Tanner Canyon circling the bases of the Escalante and Cardenas Buttes, which were named after the first white men to enter this country. The camping is at-large as there are no designated sites on this unmaintained trail.

BEAMER TRAIL

An extension of the Tanner Trail up along the Colorado River is referred to as the Beamer Trail. This is an improved Indian footpath named for Ben Beamer who was an early prospector and miner. The trail passes the Comanche and Palisades Creeks and reaches the confluence of the Little Colorado River below the Palisades of the Desert.

It is in this area that the copper mining operations took place in the late 1800's. There are many scattered, historic Indian ruins as well as old mining artifacts. These should be left exactly where they are to authenticate their existance. State and Federal laws prohibit their removal.

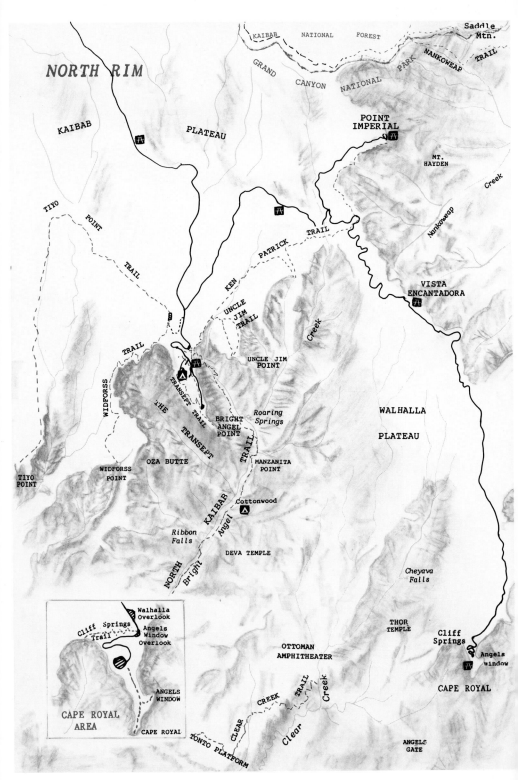

NORTH RIM

KAIBAB NATIONAL FOREST

Saddle Mtn.

GRAND CANYON NATIONAL PARK

NANKOWEAP TRAIL

KAIBAB PLATEAU

POINT IMPERIAL

MT. HAYDEN

Nankoweap Creek

TIYO POINT TRAIL

KEN PATRICK TRAIL

VISTA ENCANTADORA

UNCLE JIM TRAIL

UNCLE JIM POINT

Creek

WIDFORSS TRAIL

THE TRANSEPT TRAIL

BRIGHT ANGEL POINT

Roaring Springs

WALHALLA PLATEAU

OZA BUTTE

WIDFORSS POINT

MANZANITA POINT

TIYO POINT

KAIBAB TRAIL

Cottonwood

Angel

Ribbon Falls

DEVA TEMPLE

Cheyava Falls

NORTH Bright

THOR TEMPLE

Cliff Springs

Angels Window

CAPE ROYAL

Walhalla Overlook

Cliff Springs Trail

Angels Window Overlook

OTTOMAN AMPHITHEATER

Clear Creek

ANGELS GATE

ANGELS WINDOW

CAPE ROYAL AREA

CAPE ROYAL

CLEAR CREEK TRAIL

Clear

TONTO PLATFORM

40

NORTH RIM

The road leading to the North Rim of the Grand Canyon passes through one of the most beautiful forest lands of the west. Situated on the high domed limestone Kaibab Plateau (8000'-9000'), the virgin pine and spruce forest is one of the largest unbroken stretches on the continent being some fifty miles long and thirty miles wide. Its remoteness has preserved it through the years from excessive timbering. Its natural beauty and ecological system has been maintained.

Once this plateau was the home of the Paiute Indians. They hunted for the plentiful game found in the forest and gathered the edible plants found in the meadows. Many ruins and scattered artifacts have been discovered throughout the Plateau area. Some wild horses have been sighted, and are believed to be the descendants of those who broke away from the Paiutes long ago.

It is now the home of an endemic species, the Kaibab squirrel. With tasseled ears and a large all-white bushy tail, it is a cousin of the Abert squirrel found in the pinyon-juniper forests of the South Rim and northern Arizona. Surrounded by desert, river and impenetrable cliffs, these unique squirrels have remained isolated to keep their species intact.

The approach road to the North Rim winds through the ponderosa pines, tall Engelmann spruce, and Douglas fir intermixed with magnificent groves of tall, white columns of aspens, and shrubs. Grasses and wildflowers such as the Indian paintbrush, red and lavender thistle, and lupine add their color throughout the seasons. Even the stalwart presense of the yellow or brown stalks of the common mullein with their gray-green leaves add their glory.

In the autumn when the aspen leaves turn to gold contrasting with the blue spruce and fir trees, the buff grasses and purple asters make the drive through the forest and meadows especially rewarding. The squirrels and chipmunks can be seen as they scurry about and wild turkeys are found along the road. The Kaibab mule deer feed in the meadow usually in the early morning or late afternoon and into the night.

Being higher in elevation than the South Rim, various ecological communities are represented on the Kaibab Plateau. At the bottom of the Inner Canyon, hot desert temperatures reach over 100° with desert plants and wildlife. As the elevation and climate change with each stratified formation up to the Kaibab Limestone, so does the ecological community change. The temperatures reaching far below zero in winter on the high North Rim plateau, corresponding with that of a northern Canadian environment, a spruce and fir community with different animals and plants is found.

It is an interesting phenomenon that a winter visitor can be in freezing six-foot, snow-covered North Rim, then go down the North Kaibab Trail for eight miles, and less than a half-mile in elevation to find a warm, desert environmant with flowers blooming.

KAIBAB MULE DEER

The mule deer of the Kaibab National Forest distinguished themselves not by being a different species or having a different appearance, but in their distinction of undergoing a natural management program.

In the early 1900's, President Theodore Roosevelt established a Federal Game Refuge for hunters in the Kaibab Forest. When the predators were exterminated and the livestock of sheep and cattle were removed from the region, the deer population rapidly increased with the prevailing ecological balance disrupted.

As time went on this became a serious problem. Deer were everywhere eating shrubs, trees, and generally overgrazing the land. By 1924 over 100,000 deer were in the Refuge. The Forest Service and Wildlife agencies became alarmed. While the problem was in the state and federal courts determining the best way to eliminate the excessive amount of deer, the deer solved their dilemna.

As their food became scarce they starved to death, and instinctively developed a lower reproductive rate. This scientific phenomenon is called 'irruption'. By 1940 the deer population was reduced to only 10,000.

Aspen Stand in Kaibab National Forest   *Connie Rudd*

Grand Canyon Lodge   Lewis Clark

ACCOMMODATIONS AND SERVICES

The magnificent Grand Canyon Lodge rising up from the canyon wall is a grand old stone and log structure. It was built on the rim near Bright Angel Point by the Utah Parks Company after a fire in 1932 razed the original North Rim Inn that was built in 1929. The present lodge was completed in 1937.

The lodge has a lounge overlooking the Bright Angel Canyon and a veranda with chairs. The large picture windows in the lovely dining room offer a spectacular panoramic view. The Reservation Desk and National Park Service Information Desk is in the lobby. Literature is on sale there. Evening programs are held in the Recreation Room. There is a Western Saloon, Buffeteria and Snack Bar, Sun Room, Curio and Gift Shop, Post Office, and First-Aid Station.

The attractive cabins nestled under the aspens and pines around the main building are made of natural stone and timbers taken from the Kaibab Forest. Some of the cabins have excellent canyon views.

The Ranger Naturalist programs are conducted in the lodge and in the amphitheater by the campground. Nature and geology walks and talks are given twice daily as well as evening programs until October 15th. Church services include the Roman Catholic, Protestant, and Church of Jesus Christ of Latter-Day Saints. Guided bus and auto tours are available to Cape Royal and Point Imperial. Mule tours to the Inner Canyon and horseback riding can be arranged.

The Ranger Station with the Backcountry Reservation Office is near the campground. The North Rim Campground is on a first-come, first-serve basis. Reservations are accepted for groups of six or more. Write to Group Reservation, North Rim, Grand Canyon, Ariz. 86023. The Camper Store, service station, laundry and showers are situated near the campground. The North Rim Pub and Game Room is next to the store. Propane is available only at Jacob Lake.

NORTH RIM TRAILS

The Bright Angel Point Trail, a half-mile descent from the Grand Canyon Lodge parking area takes about a half-hour for the round trip. A path leading from the Lodge meets the trail. From the Point (8145') is a vast panorama of temples, buttes, crags of endless tints and shades which change with the time and weather. From here it is a good place to watch the early morning sun rise lighting up the canyons below, or in the evening to see the sun set and the canyons become dark as the heavens become a gorgeous array of color.

There is a self-guiding tour out to the Point and the Ranger Naturalist programs include a geology and nature walk-talk twice daily along the trail. Benches are placed conveniently to rest or contemplate the view.

The 1.5 mile Transept Trail begins at the campground and follows along the western rim to the Grand Canyon Lodge. For a loop trip, the return to the campground can be made along the Bridle Path on the eastern rim which parallels the road.

The Widforss Trail is ten miles and a five-hour round trip journey winding through the forest and along the North Rim at the head of the Transept. From the overlook there is a panorama of the western buttes, temples, and colorful formations. Swallows, swifts, and ravens dart about to soar in the warm updrafts coming from the canyons below. The unique Kaibab squirrels are commonly seen along the trail. The trailhead and parking lot is reached by the dirt road which is one-fourth mile south of the Cape Royal Road.

Both the Uncle Jim and Ken Patrick Trails follows through the forest northeast from the North Kaibab Trail parking lot. The 5.0 mile Uncle Jim Trail takes about a half day for the entire trip. The trail leads out to a point to overlook the North Kaibab Trail switchbacks and down into Roaring Springs Canyon.

The Ken Patrick Trail is twelve miles long and takes six hours at least one way. From the parking lot the trail passes the head of Roaring Springs Canyon. After crossing the creek it continues to the head of Bright Angel Canyon junctioning with the Old Kaibab Trail leading to the Phantom Ranch. From there the trail proceeds east through a heavy forest with glades that support many wildflowers and wildlife. After passing the upper Bright Angel Creek, the trail crosses the Cape Royal Road to follow the rim at the head of the impressive Nankoweap Canyon, west of Sullivan Peak, and out to Point Imperial. There is no camping allowed on either of these two trails.

East From Point Imperial   MAC

44

Angel's Window   MAC

CAPE ROYAL TOUR

One of the most pleasant and rewarding trips in all of Grand Canyon is the one day journey to Point Imperial and down the Walhalla Plateau to Cape Royal. This 67-mile round trip has picnic sites at several places along the route, inspiring overlooks and an intimate drive on the winding two-way road through the pine, juniper, aspen, fir, spruce, and Gambel oak trees and flowers and shrubs blooming in their season.

The three-mile road extending out to Point Imperial follows along the upper end of Bright Angel Creek and then climbs eastward up to the Point (8803'), the highest location on the North Rim. From various overlooks is a truly breathtaking vista encompassing the land of color and light. The sweeping panorama includes the Vermilion Cliffs to the north, Saddle and Navajo Mountains, Navajo Indian Reservation and Painted Desert country to the east with the shifting shadows in multi-hued brilliance of the Marble Platform. The expanive Nankoweap Canyon and Creek is below. The Cape Royal Bus Tour which leaves the Grand Canyon Lodge daily makes this scenic wonder a regular stop.

Vista Encantadora at 8500' offers what the name implies - an awesome, enchanted view of colorful buttes, peaks, and down into the Nankoweap Canyon to the Colorado River.

Traveling south on the Plateau to the end at Cape Royal the road is bordered with shrubs and flowers in the meadows. There is a comfort station and a picnic area at the end of the road. Trails lead to Angels Window, Cliff Springs, and out to the cape (7865'). Markers along the Nature Trail to the various overlooks interpret the natural history. Benches are provided for rest and contemplation.

The forty-mile view from Cape Royal includes Freya Castle, Wotans Throne, Vishnu Temple and down Vishnu Creek. Southward is the escarpment of the South Rim with the San Francisco Mountains in the distance. The shimmering Colorado River is below. A noble sight indeed, with colors changing with the passing sun and clouds.

Prehistoric Indians inhabited the Walhalla Plateau with evidences of ruins found along the roads, meadows and at Cliff Springs. The one-mile trail down to Cliff Springs starts across the road from the Angel Window Overlook and winds through the forest canyon to the rim. The Indian dwellings were mostly destroyed some years ago. Cattle rustlers held up at the Springs and trampled over the footpaths and artifacts left by the early Indians with disregard for their historical significence. (Do not drink the water from the Springs as it is unsafe.)

45

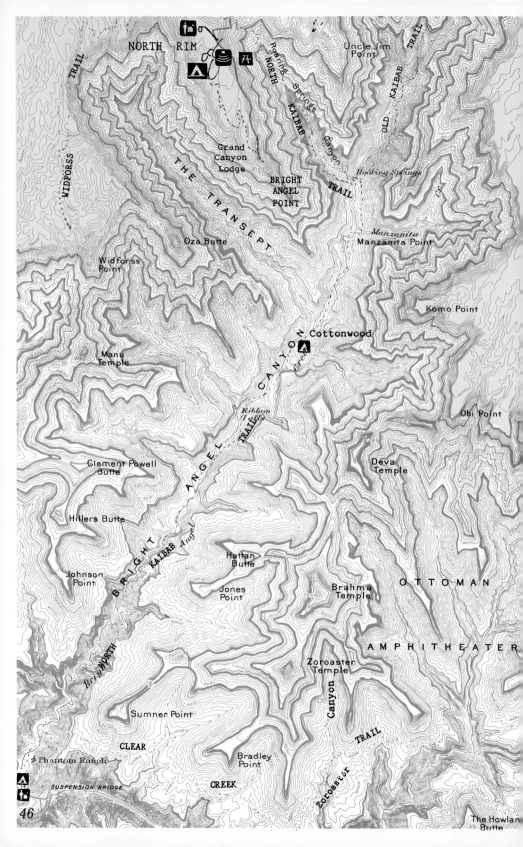

Looking Down Bright Angel Canyon   MAC

NORTH KAIBAB TRAIL

The descent from the North Rim down to the Colorado River is over a mile in elevation and some fourteen miles by trail. It follows along the Bright Angel Creek most of the way. The trailhead starts 2.0 miles north of the Grand Canyon Lodge at the head of Roaring Springs Canyon. The Old Kaibab Trail took off further east at the upper end of Bright Angel Creek. Washouts after storms and heavy snow-melting crumbled the trail making it hard to find. It is now partly overgrown in sections, but an experienced hiker, with scrambling can find the way.

The fault fracture of the Bright Angel Canyon as in Garden Creek south and across the River from it, created breaks in the cliffs resulting in an easy access route down into the Inner Canyon. Anasazi Indians traveled on this natural trail to their gardens and water supply, as did prospectors looking for gold, and explorers who came later to survey the land.

The trail sharply descends the Roaring Springs Canyon with switchbacks through the Coconino formation. The only section of the trail that had to be blasted out, the Supai Tunnel was made about fifty years ago when the present route replaced the Old Bright Angel Trail. During the years floods have washed out the trail in various sections. Bridges have been constructed to preserve as much of the trail as possible. However, the force of water rushing down each spring and flood periods makes it difficult to maintain a permanently built trail.

With the descent passing through several Life Zone ecosystems the pine, spruce, and juniper forest gives way to a dryer, more desert environment. This becomes quite evident as the trail reaches the massive Redwall Limestone formation. With water seepage through the rocks and gravel, some shrubs, trees and flowers have been able to survive in the warmer climate.

Roaring Springs, near the confluence of Bright Angel and Roaring Springs Canyons, is an ideal 10.0 mile, one-day round trip for the hardy hiker. Mule train tours go down this far on the trail for their one-day trip making the traffic extremely heavy at times. One-day hikes can be made also as far as Coconino Overlook (2.5 miles round trip); a longer trip to Supai Tunnel and return (3.5 miles round trip);or down to the Redwall Bridge (4.5 miles round trip). Roaring Springs Canyon is the most strenuous part of the entire journey. The trail levels off to a slower descent as it goes down along the Bright Angel Creek.

Cottonwood Campground (7.0 miles from the trailhead) is a beautiful oasis with bright green leaves of the welcoming trees shimmering. With this shade from the burning sun it is a true respite from the dusty, rocky trail. In the early 1930's mule tours visited this old Indian site, and pioneers, prospectors and explorers rested in the cool shade of the cottonwoods. With sufficient water from the creek, the trees have grown to be a most hospitable sight to the traveler. Some evidences have been found where the Anasazi Indians probably grew crops here.

Situated at the point where the Transept and Bright Angel Canyon meet, the views from the campground are outstanding. Obi Butte and Manu Temple are above to the west with Obi Point and Deva Temple to the east. There are tables, restrooms, and Ranger Station. Reservations are needed to secure space as there are only a limited number of sites available. The restrooms and Ranger Station are closed from November through April. Winter camping is allowed with a reduced number of spaces. There are no supplies or services here.

Ribbon Falls with the calcium carbonate of the limestone creating the travertine pools support delicate ferns and moss that hugs the banks by the falls. These pools are similar to those found in Havasu Canyon. This is a precious area where no camping is allowed. With the constant flowing of Bright Angel Creek, wildlife and wildflowers flourish, although just beyond the moisture of the creek, the desert environment is prevalent.

In The Box section the way becomes quite jagged with the trail narrowing. More bridges are needed to ease the many creek crossings to get through the ancient rock formation. The vertical walls of the Tapeats Sandstone and Vishnu Group are exposed and worn down by faulting, uplifts, and erosion.

After junctioning with the Clear Creek Trail heading east, the Phantom Ranch and Bright Angel Campground are just beyond before reaching the Colorado River.

CLEAR CREEK TRAIL

The trail to Clear Creek starts about a half-mile north of Phantom Ranch. It skirts around the cliffs above the Colorado River on the Tonto Platform. It is a good one-day trip out of Bright Angel Campground or from the Ranch. Once inhabited by the ancient ones, there are numerous ruins and sites in this general area and along Clear Creek. Caves in the rocks are in several canyons. From the trail some temple climbing and canyon exploring is possible.

Cheyava Falls, the highest in the Park, is reached by some scrambling up Clear Creek as no specific trail follows up the creek to the base of the falls. This beautiful cascading series of falls from the Redwall Limestone formation were first discovered by the Kolb brothers in 1908.

From the North Kaibab Trail it is 8.7 miles to Clear Creek with no water along the trail. The cross-country trail down to the Colorado River from the end of the Clear Creek Trail is about a 6.0 mile round trip. This area is closed to camping.

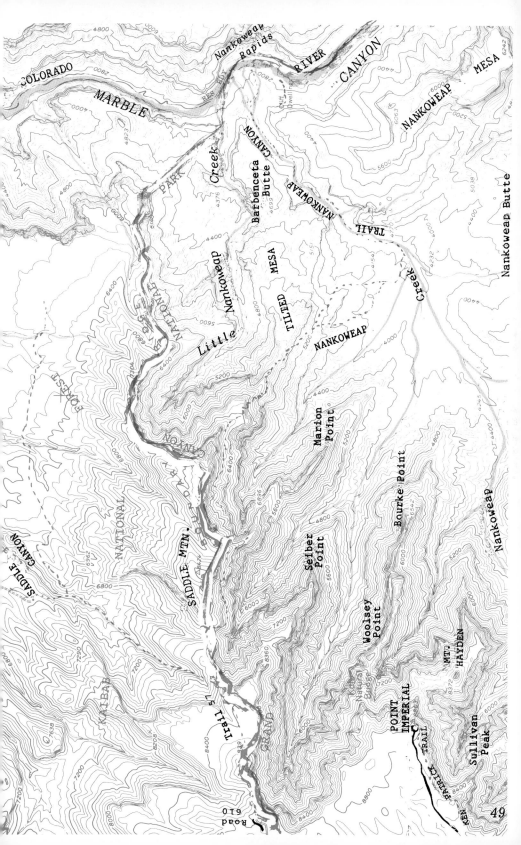

COLORADO

MARBLE

RIVER   CANYON

Nankoweap   Rapids

NANKOWEAP   MESA

6242

Creek

4376

CANYON

Barbenceta Butte
4699

NANKOWEAP

PARK

4823

6063

5200

TRAIL

5038

Nankoweap Butte

NATIONAL

Little   Nankoweap

TILTED   MESA

NANKOWEAP

515

Creek

4232

4245

4400

FOREST

CANYON

Marion
Point

Bourke
Point
6542

Nankoweap

SADDLE CANYON

NATIONAL

6962

Seiber
Point

BOUNDARY

SADDLE MTN.

6896

Woolsey
Point

6800

KAIBAB

Nankweap
Bridge

MT.
HAYDEN
8372

Trail 57

POINT
IMPERIAL
8803

GRAND

Sullivan
Peak

8208

PATRICK   TRAIL

KEN

8400

Road 610

49

NANKOWEAP TRAIL

Western River Expeditions

The 14.0 mile descent south and eastward down to the Colorado River via the Nankoweap Trail starts west of Saddle Mountain (8424') on the Boundary Ridge. Forest Service roads reach the Saddle Mountain trailhead. From the west, a fire-road #610 follows the border of the National Forest and the National Park to meet the Forest Service trail #57. This trail passes through the pine and juniper forest for 3.0 miles to reach the trailhead for the Nankoweap Trail.

In 1960 some 8000 acres burned in the Saddle Mountain area which was set off by lightning. There are some dry slopes, but generally the land has been rejuvenated with thick groves of beautiful aspens.

From the north the dirt road off Hwy.89A to Buffalo Ranch and Saddle Mountain meets the Forest Service trail that goes south for 2.0 miles. This trail climbs through a beautiful ponderosa pine forest to junction with the trail #57 coming from the west. From the Nankoweap Saddle are extensive views of the rugged crags, steep canyons, and the colorful basin below.

After following along the bench, the trail switchbacks down through the Supai formation to the west of Tilted Mesa, entering the open valley looking south to the Nankoweap Butte (5430') and the magnificent red crags reaching up to the Nankoweap Mesa (6242'). At Nankoweap Creek the trail veers northeast through the red cliffs that flank the narrow Nankoweap Canyon, to the Colorado River about the rapids.

The trail is washed out in sections and some experience in backcountry scrambling is necessary in locating the route. It is in the Primitive Management Zone with no facilities or maintained trail. Camping is at-large. From looking at the photograph opposite, the country is open and exposed. Temperatures are high in the summer, so spring and fall travel is recommended. Water is available from Nankoweap Creek or at the Colorado River.

From the sandbar at the River, it is possible to reach by trail the Indian cliff dwellings where the 'ancient ones' lived and stored their food. They cultivated crops up on the terrace and on the river-watered floor below. The dwellings beneath the overhanging cliffs were built up from rocks to form enclosures. The trail to the dwellings can be seen in the photograph opposite, which was taken some 35,000' above the canyon.

The trail leading eastward from the Forest Service dirt road at Saddle Mountain proceeds through junipers and pinyon pines to reach the impressive Marble Canyon overlook. The panorama includes magnificent multi-colored cliffs and formations, deep canyons, and northeast to the Navajo Indian Reservation and Painted Desert.

NORTH RIM TO JACOB LAKE

From the North Rim Entrance Station to and including Jacob Lake there are many recreational opportunities for summer and winter. There are lodges and campgrounds, nature walks, Forest Service trails for hiking or horsebacking, hunting in season and various winter sport activities such as snowmobiling, sledding, Nordic cross-country skiing, or just playing in the snow.

From Hwy.67 roads lead west to Big Springs and Indian Hollow, and east to the Saddle Mountain area. The unspoiled and scenic backcountry is an uncrowded wilderness. There are no services or water on these roads so the traveler must be prepared for all conditions and emergencies. Remember no bikes or jeeps are allowed over the grassland meadows, only snowmobiles as they do not harm the meadows for the animals or create erosive damage.

It is possible to camp at-large in Kaibab National Forest. Certain rules must apply for environmental reasons. No camping is allowed in the meadows or along the highways or back roads. All fires must be extinguished; all human waste buried; and all litter cleared away from the camping aite. It is advisable to inform friends and relatives of your destination and when to expect your return. Be sure to check the condition of the roads and weather before venturing out too far.

At Jacob Lake (7900'), 30 miles from the North Entrance Station, the Inn offers lodging, trailer spaces, grocery store and bakery, gift shop, cafe, and gas station with propane. (No propane sold at the North Rim.) The Forest Service maintains a nice campground under the forest cover with a dump station for trailers, but no hook-ups; tables and grills. It is open from May to October. At Jacob Lake there is a Visitor Center for information and Nature programs and walks.

At Kaibab, five miles north of the Park Entrance (8800') the Kaibab Lodge (8000'), open from May to September, has a restaurant, curio and gift shop. The North Rim Country Store has gas as well as supplies. They arrange tours for mule rides and float-boat trips down the Colorado River. They close mid-November. The Forest Service maintains the DeMotte Park Campground, which has tables and grills, but no hook-ups.

ALL ROADS ARE CLOSED IN WINTER DUE TO HEAVY SNOWSTORMS.

Kaibab Forest   MAC

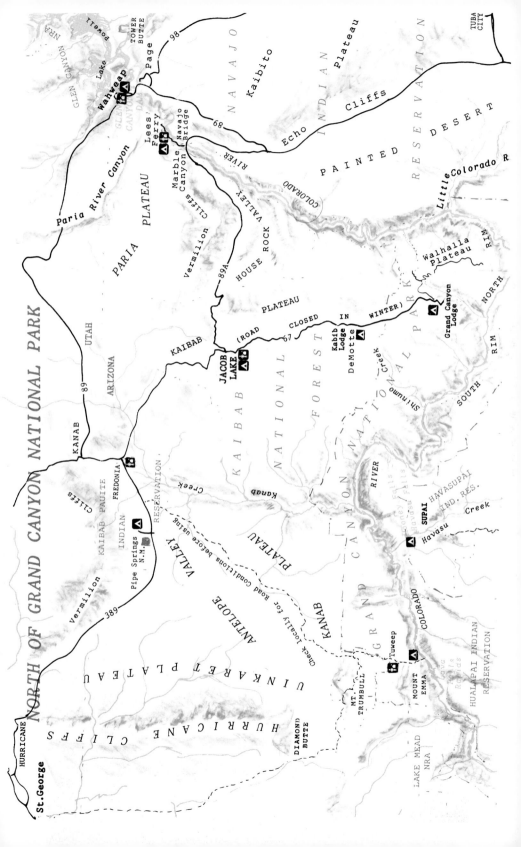

NORTH OF GRAND CANYON NATIONAL PARK

NRA

GLEN CANYON

Lake Powell

TOWER BUTTE

Wahweap

GLEN CANYON DAM

Page

98

NAVAJO

Kaibito

INDIAN

Plateau

Echo

Cliffs

TUBA CITY

68

Lees Ferry

Marble Canyon

Navajo Bridge

COLORADO

RIVER

PAINTED

RESERVATION

DESERT

Little Colorado R

Little

COLORADO

Paria River Canyon

Vermilion Cliffs

PARIA PLATEAU

PARIA

89A

HOUSE ROCK VALLEY

Walhalla Plateau

NORTH RIM

RIM

Grand Canyon Lodge

PLATEAU

UTAH

ARIZONA

89

KAIBAB

(ROAD CLOSED IN WINTER)

67

Kaibab Lodge

DeMotte

Shinumo Creek

SOUTH RIM

JACOB LAKE

KANAB

FREDONIA

KAIBAB PAIUTE INDIAN RESERVATION

Pipe Springs N.M.

Creek

KAIBAB

NATIONAL

FOREST

Kanab

PLATEAU

RIVER

Mooney Falls

HAVASUPAI IND. RES.

SUPAI

Havasu

Creek

CLIFFS

Vermilion

389

ANTELOPE VALLEY

check locally for road conditions before using

KANAB PLATEAU

GRAND

CANYON

NATIONAL

PARK

COLORADO

HURRICANE

St.George

UINKARET PLATEAU

HURRICANE CLIFFS

DIAMOND BUTTE

MT. TRUMBULL

Tuweep

MOUNT EMMA

Lava Falls Rapids

LAKE MEAD NRA

HUALAPAI INDIAN RESERVATION

TOROWEAP VALLEY-TUWEEP

West of Fredonia off Hwy.389, the 56-mile graded dirt road leads south through Antelope Valley to Tuweep and Toroweap Valley. From the west the unimproved 90-mile road leads south and east from St. George. Quill Road passes Hurricane Cliffs and on to Main Street Valley, past Mt. Trumbull Wilderness Area meeting the road from Fredonia before entering the Toroweap Valley. Mt. Trumbull (8028') and Mt. Emma (7698') stand out. There are some mineral explorations with equipment using this road.

These approaches are in remote areas with no telephones or assistance in emergencies, no gas, water or food services. The roads are not advisable for trailers or motor homes. When wet with snow or rain the roads become impassable. Be sure to carry extra water for your vehicle as well as yourself. Be sure to let someone know of your destination.

The Toroweap Valley-Tuweep-Vulcan's Throne area was once part of Grand Canyon National Monument but in 1975 it became part of Grand Canyon National Park. Six miles south of the Ranger Station at Tuweep is a primitive campground. Permits must be obtained at the Backcountry Reservation Office on the South Rim or at Tuweep Ranger Station.

Here in this remote wilderness is a magnificent display of volcanic action which sprewed debris over boulders, benches, and cliffs. The spectacular and dramatic views are of the deep and narrow walls of the gorge and the Colorado River 3000' below. The great walls of the canyon were carved through the centuries. The tremendous eruptive forces that occurred later in time, created the total beauty we see today. Lava dams, resulting from the eruptions have been cut through by the turbulent river leaving huge boulders like the Vulcan's Anvil, shown below. Smaller boulders make the white waters of the Lava Falls Rapids treacherous and formidible.

Vulcan's Throne is a beautiful 600' high cinder cone that sits at the edge of the rim on top of the Toroweap Fault. From here the views are awesome with the muddy waters below, to the sheer vertical cliffs with hardened lave-flow ledges and talus slopes, to the Prospect Valley and Auberry Cliffs to the south.

The trail to Lava Falls Rapids (1.5 mile) starting at the western base of Vulcan's Throne descends 2800' on the old lava flow route to the river. The trail is rough and steep. It takes about a hour to go down but about four hours to return.

Vulcan's Anvil   Western River Expeditions

John Cummings

PIPE SPRINGS NATIONAL MONUMENT

   For a visit to the American past of cowboys and their colorful, yet hard-working life in the Mormon frontier days, see Pipe Springs National Monument. It is about 14 miles southwest of Fredonia, off Hwy. 389.

   A constant flowing spring in the dry Arizona land was used first by prehistoric pueblo Indians, later by the nomadic Paiutes who camped and hunted in this area. Then came the Mormon missionaries in the 1860's and settled. There is a guided tour of the historic Winsor Castle and the other buildings that are made of native materials, the corral, gardens, and orchard. The many preserved rooms in the castle along with their pioneer furnishings depict their frontier living. The memorabilia of the cowboys and their tools, equipment, and lifestyle are well displayed. The Visitor Center has exhibits and offer assistance and travel information.

HONEYMOON TRAIL

Take a journey into the past. Experience the life of the pioneers. The Honeymoon Trail follows the one taken by the many Mormon couples who went from their Arizona settlement west to St. George to receive a proper Mormon wedding in the temple.

This overland, covered-wagon adventure travels past the beautiful Vermilion Cliffs, over grasslands, mesas, and sage-covered deserts to allow the traveler an intimate relationship with nature. Taste meals the way the pioneers prepared them. Sleep in the wagons, or tents, or under the skies in the cool nights.

Starting at Kanab, Utah, the Honeymoon Trail Company has several trips each summer for this covered-wagon trek. It takes five days to reach St. George. Safety is assured with sturdy wagons, well-trained horses, experienced wranglers and Trail Boss. For further information contact Honeymoon Trail Company, Moccasin, Arizona, 86022.

KAIBAB PAUITE INDIAN RESERVATION

The Kaibab Pauite Indian Reservation is situated high on the pinyon pine-juniper mesa within the shadows of beautiful multi-colored strated Vermilion Cliffs, and overlooks the open sage-strewn Antelope Valley to the south. To the east across the Kanab Creek is the Kaibab dome-shaped plateau country. For a peaceful, one-with-nature interlude in motor home or trailer traveling, stay at the Kaibab-Paiute Campground. It is just one-fourth mile up from the Pipe Springs Visitor Center. There are complete hook-ups, tables, tent camping areas, with fire rings and water, free showers, a laundromat, and general store open in the summer. The fees are reasonable.

A path to the past is at the campground with old Paiute Indian winter and summer shelters situated among the Mormon tea and shrubs, pinyon pines and junipers. Nearby are Educational Hiking Trails for good evening family walks.

It is important to remember that this or any other Indian reservation is their home and we are guests. Consideration must be given for their privacy and property.

Remember when driving on unimproved backcountry roads that have no services or anyone to assist in emergencies, discretion is important as well as knowing your vehicle. The wear and tear on any vehicle from the jeep or unpaved roads is far greater than on freeways.

Ancient Paiute Indian Dwelling   MAC

Colorado River From Navajo Bridge   MAC

NORTH OF PARK - EAST

Fredonia, the headquarters for the North Kaibab National Forest, has some accommodations and services for travelers.

Leaving the high mesa, sage-covered plateau country east of Fredonia, Hwy. 89A casually climbs up through the pinyon pine and juniper forest. The road parallels the south rim of the LeFevre Canyon to reach the top of the dome-like Kaibab Plateau and Jacob Lake. This is a scenic drive with cliffrose, Gambel oaks, tall ponderosa pines, pinyons and junipers, and wildflowers enhancing the roadside.

East of Jacob Lake and the North Rim junction, Hwy. 89A descends through canyons and curves to the eastern edge of the plateau. Some years ago there were white crosses placed off the road at sharp bends which were memorials to those who had lost their life at that point. The first glimpse of the vast House Rock Valley and the colorful Vermilion Cliffs beyond is at Valley View, about a mile from the National Forest border. It is a great contrast to see the pastel painted lands after driving through the verdant Kaibab Forest.

At the bottom of the hill the House Rock Valley Road (gravel) leads north to meet Hwy. 89. Five miles east is the junction for the 20-mile dirt road leading south to Buffalo Ranch, where the great bison roam free between the canyon desert and the high plateau country. From this road it is possible to proceed south to reach Saddle Mountain, the boundary ridge region of the National Park and National Forest, and the Nankoweap Trail going down to the Colorado River.

Accommodations on Hwy. 89A are at Cliff Dwellers Lodge, Vermilion Cliff Lodge, and Marble Canyon (3603'), all in the foreground of the magnificent, impressive Vermilion Cliffs.

Marble Canyon offers a trading post with fishing tackle and camera supplies, restaurant, and gas for automobiles and boats. There is a memorial plaque for Dominquez Y Escalante and models of Navajo hogans. From here the road goes north for five miles to Lees Ferry.

The highway continues east to the great steel span called the Navajo Bridge which rises 467' above the Marble Canyon and the Colorado River. The span is 616' long. A picnic area with shade and viewpoint enables the visitor to look down the sheer vertical redwall cliffs to the river far below.

57

LEES FERRY   *MAC*

October 26, 1776. When the Founding Fathers were fighting in New York with Great Britian for our independence, Fray Silvestre Velez de Escalante, along with his superior Fray Atanasio Dominquez camped on the banks of the Colorado River where the Paria River joins it, near the present site of Lees Ferry. Escalante wrote in his diary:

> *" It is a bend completely surrounded by very high cliffs and crests of red earth of various formations; and since the intervening plain below is of the same color, it has an agreebly confused appearance."*

The expedition party remained in this area for about a week trying to locate a safe and easy ford across the Colorado River. They were the first white men to see and explore this country. It would be about a hundred years later before Major John Powell, Jacob Hamblin, John Doyle Lee and other Mormon missionaries came to the confluence of the Paria River and the Colorado River.

Major Powell and his party camped on the banks where he had a supply base. They had explored the area prior to their second River trip. They crossed the river in an improvised boat then climbed up and over Echo Cliffs to the Kaibito Plateau to reach 'The Ancient Pueblos in the Provence of Tusayan', or Hopi villages of Oraibi and neighboring towns. It was here Powell first became interested in their cultural and ancestral backgrounds.

Before the Navajo Bridge was completed in 1929 to span the River, the crossing for Mormon pioneers going south to colonize the Arizona territory was by ferry. John Lee, a Mormon with nineteen wives, and a fugitive who later was convicted and shot for the part he allegedly played in the Mountain Meadows Massacre, established the ferry in 1871. The cabin at Lonely Dell where he may have lived in still stands as well as the remains of the old orchard and plowed fields. Another historical building here is Lee's Ferry Fort which was built in 1874 ostensibly as a trading post for the Navajo Indians.

When the pioneers crossed the river, it was adventuresome enough, but when they climbed up on the rugged, rocky shelf known as Lee's Backbone, it must have been horrendous. Some wagon ruts can still be seen in the rocks. Later, the Dugway was constructed to bypass this rough, most difficult route to reach the upper bench.

Lees Ferry   MAC

GOLD! The quest for gold was in the hearts and dreams of men everywhere in the early 1900's. Charles H. Spencer's dream became as thin and slim as the quality of the gold he found here. The only traces left today sitting out in the desert sun is the old boiler and hull of his steamboat he used to transport coal for his pumps. However, all the coal brought down the river from Warm Creek was needed to operate the steamboat with nothing left for the processing of the gold.

In the Lees Ferry area there are diversified recreational opportunities with trail hiking, fishing for trout, boat trips, viewing old ruins of historical significence, or just relaxing in the warm desert sun among the beautiful and colorful cliffs. There is a National Park Ranger Station, a campground with some cabanas, picnic area, and boat launching ramp.

An interesting boat trip is available which winds up the Colorado River as it bends and twists for fifteen miles to the base of the imposing Glen Canyon Dam and under the great steel bridge where Hwy. 89 crosses the River in front of the dam. The water is quite calm on this side of the dam and passing through the canyon between sheer walls of the cliffs to meet the sheer wall of the dam is exhilerating.

Lees Ferry is the departure point for the exciting adventure trip down the Colorado River through Grand Canyon National Park.

Getting Ready for the River Run Down The Colorado River   MAC

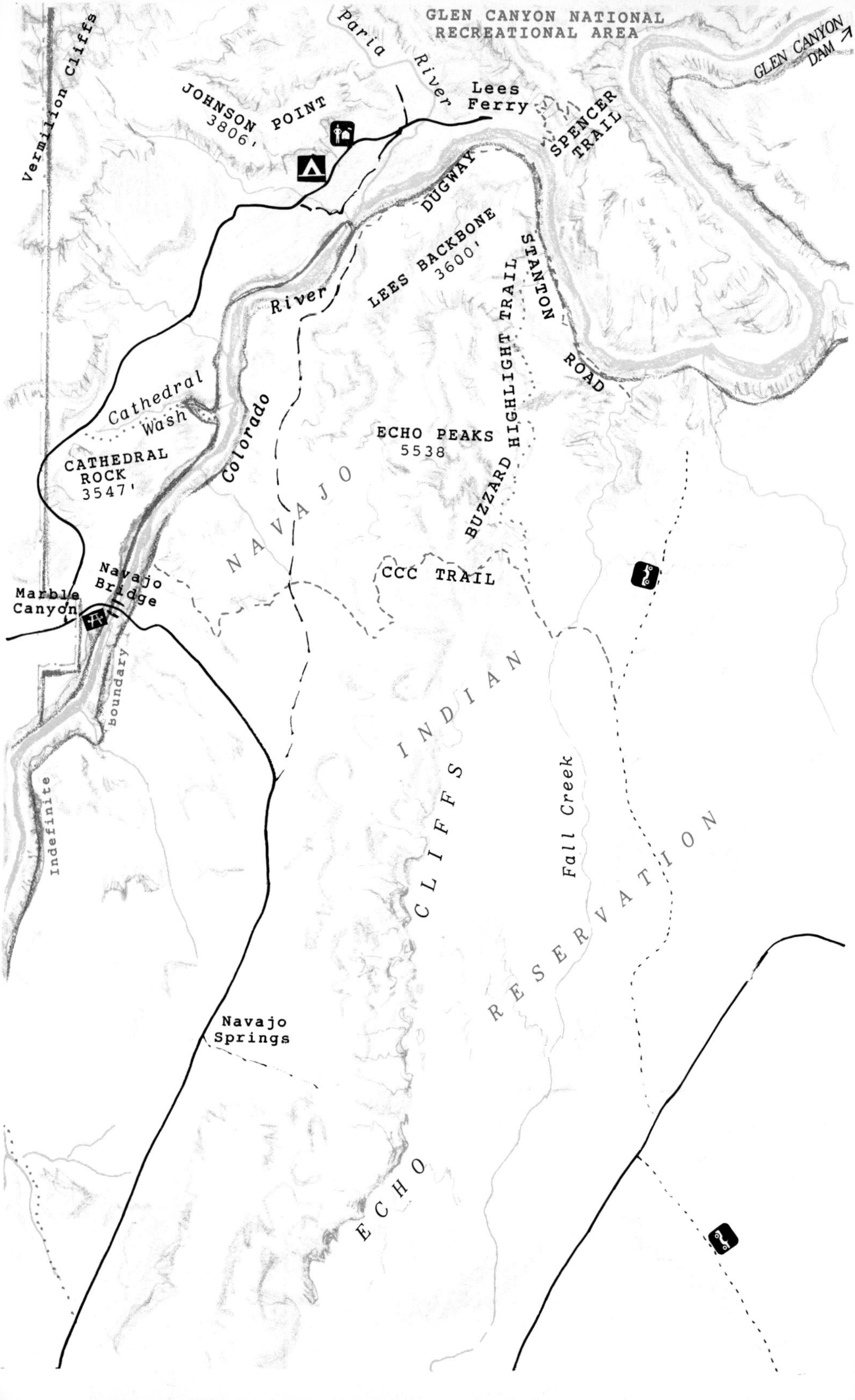

GLEN CANYON NATIONAL
RECREATIONAL AREA

GLEN CANYON
DAM

Vermilion Cliffs

Paria River

Lees
Ferry

JOHNSON POINT
3806'

SPENCER
TRAIL

DUGWAY

LEES BACKBONE
3600'

STANTON
ROAD

River

BUZZARD HIGHLIGHT TRAIL

Cathedral
Wash

Colorado

ECHO PEAKS
5538

CATHEDRAL
ROCK
3547'

N A V A J O

CCC TRAIL

Navajo
Bridge

Marble
Canyon

I N D I A N

Boundary

C L I F F S

Fall Creek

R E S E R V A T I O N

Indefinite

Navajo
Springs

E C H O

LEES FERRY TRAILS
MAC

There are a number of trails at Lees Ferry. Because of the dry, hot desert conditions with little available shade, it is advisable to travel in the spring or fall to best enjoy the beauty and the experience. In the summer there could be flash-floods from the thunderstorms in some areas. It is necessary to get permission from the Navajo Indian Tribe to hike on any trail in their reservation.

SPENCER TRAIL: The trail leads up above the old steamboat ruins of Charles Spencer, over the Chinle formation to reach the mesa some 1700' above. From here there are excellent views of the River and the colorful Echo Cliffs to the south.

CCC TRAIL: Built in the 1930's, this trail assisted the Navajo sheepherders in reaching the river to water their stock. It decends from the Kaibito Plateau, down the slot cut through the Echo Cliffs to reach the river some 1700' below. The trail crosses the old pioneer route, now a dirt road, leading up from the Dugway.

BUZZARD"S HIGHLINE TRAIL: Going north on the east side of Echo Peaks, this arduous trail descends the 1700' to reach the river upstream from Lees Ferry.

PARIA CANYON WILDERNESS AREA

This wilderness affords a backcountry trip through the colorful Paria Primitive Area. It is about 34 miles from Hwy.89 at the north end down to Lees Ferry. Some campsites are available but little water. The road leading to the Paria Entrance Station on Hwy.89 is between the Paria River crossing and Paradise Park. From the south, the graveled House Rock Valley Road follows north to meet Hwy.89. It is a seasonal road, and important to check both the trail and weather conditions at the time of departure into the canyon.

The trail follows the river channel with varying degrees of difficulty with some narrow cliffs and stream bed passages.

As in the Grand Canyon area, a walk through this canyon is a walk through time as the various formations of sandstone were built up some 200 million years ago. Above the Kaibab Limestone formation at the rim in Grand Canyon, more recent rock strata had been created. In the Mesozoic Era the Moekopi, Chinle, Moenave, and higher layers were formed. These rocks make up Vermilion Cliffs, Tower Butte and the red canyons surrounding Lake Powell. At Lees Ferry the yellowish Chinle formation is visibly exposed.

THE RIVER RUN

Western River Expeditions

By Donald Barnes

"After reading a magazine article and seeing the pictures, I really got the bug to go through the Grand Canyon on the Colorado River by raft, that is, in a large raft, not on a 'suicide' ride.

It was a beautiful morning in May when we all assembled at Lees Ferry. Across the river I could still see the tortuous, winding old road coming down the mountain that the pioneers used. It was nerve-racking just to think about the wagons and stagecoaches coming down that road much less than being in one.

The rafts are elongated doughnut-shaped, pointed in front. They are about 25' long and 10'wide. Attached to the base of the raft on each side, running from front to back are long, flexible 3' dismeter tubes. If the raft leans too far over to one side, the tubes would act as an 'outrigger' or pontoon and keep the raft from tipping over. The inflatable portion of the raft as well as the pontoons are made in sections so that if it is punctured, only one small portion is deflated. It was re-assuring to know that and to know that the river runners carry a gasoline-powered air pump and patching material with them. About our third day out we passed a group who had pulled their raft up on a sandbar and had removed the side pontoons to turn it over so that they could patch a hole in the main raft.

It was an 8-day trip with no supermarkets along the way so everything we needed had to be carried on the raft, and everything had to be carried back out as no debris could be left in the canyon. This is monitored very closely by the Park Rangers. Also, it was necessary to carry the facilities. It was the re-cycling kind, the same type used in airplanes and recreational vehicles. Every night it was set up at the edge of camp with a small tent erected around it, and since there was no place to knock on the door, a simple statement "anybody home" took care of any surprises.

All the food, pots, pans, plates, and cutlery were placed in waterproof boxes on collapsible racks in the center hole of the raft. Beer and soft drinks in cans were chilled by putting them in the water in a burlap bag while we floated in calm waters. That water was 'cold as ice'. It was hard to see how that water could stay so cold as only ten feet up on the bank it was uncomfortably warm. Ice was packed over the meat and stored on the racks. All of our gear - sleeping bags, clothes and personal items were placed in waterproof, rubberized bags and put on top of the supplies. These bags made a back rest for us as we sat on the sides of the raft with our feet on the pontoons.

A rope was stretched around the bags through holders which were behind us at the level of our seat. This rope was the 'life line' for going through the rapids. Just before the rapids we sat down with our feet braced against the pontoons while holding on to that life line.

The raft was equipped with a 7-horsepower outboard motor which is used primarily to manuever the raft into position to enter a rapid. The actual propelling power for the raft is the current. Some companies equip the rafts with a large motor to hurry through the calmer waters. This is like saying you have seen New York because you drove through it on the freeway.

There were two rafts on our trip, each holding 13 passengers plus the boatman and one swamper, who were also the cooks. Just before shoving off, we put on 'Mae West' life jackets as they are a requirement of the Government for everyone to wear. The boatman can not move the boat until all are equipped.

As we started our trip we could see the bottom of the river very clearly through the cold water but as we progressed we noticed the river was becoming dirtier and dirtier. Actually it was not dirt but a fine silt sand. We filled a bucket full with the water and could not see the bottom. We let it stand about five minutes and the water became clear.

Our first real sight other than the great beauty of the canyon walls and Echo Peaks was passing under the Navajo Bridge which was over 400' above us. A large semi-truck was crossing the bridge at the time and it looked like a child's toy. It is indeed a great feat of engineering.

Navajo Bridge   MAC

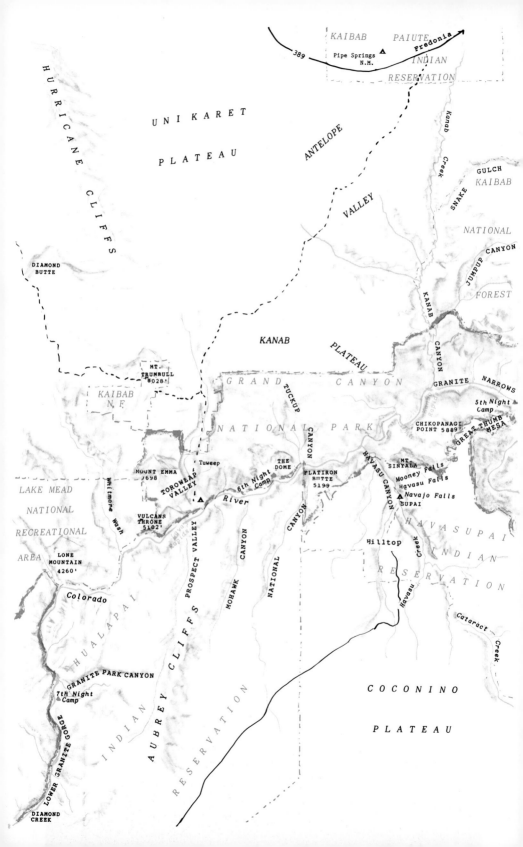

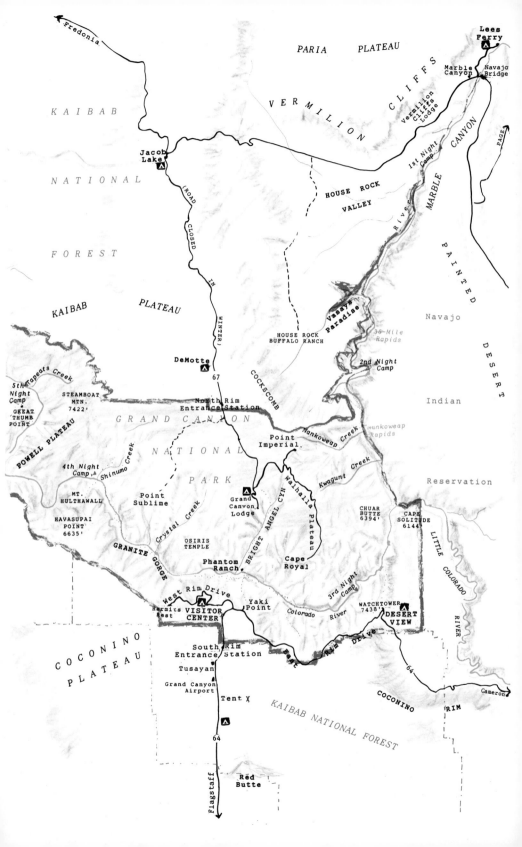

We were all settled back into our leisurely world of just drifting and looking when the boatman told us to get ready for the first rapids. This rapid was pictured on the cover of Life Magazine where fifteen people were dumped into the cold river. We took our positions and held on tight. The boatman started up the little outboard and manuevered the raft against the left bank in the deeper water with the front of the raft pointing to the center of the river. We then went into the rapids sideways and I began to question the boatman's ability. After the rapids when it was all over, I realized he was using the little outboard to push us away from the rocks. We all got wet of course, but we trembled from the joy and exhileration as well as from the cold, and looked forward to the next one.

The next event became a daily ritual before stopping for the night. The raft was beached at a given spot where there was driftwood, and everyone gathered wood and put it on the raft. We then would continue downstream to a sandbar or low ledge where we spent the night. Everyone formed a line from the raft to the camping place and all the gear, supplies, wood, etc. was unloaded by passing them from person to person. Everyone found a spot and made up their bed. Some people slept in the open on the ground under the stars, some had tube tents while my friend and I had made and taken a sleeping cot that looked like garden furniture. All of the others complained that the sand and rocks became very hard before morning.

After we all made our beds, we relaxed for a 'happy hour' and watched the cooks prepare our dinner. Such delicious meals made by the boatmen! It was my first experience with anyone who could whip up an entire meal including bread, biscuits and cake in a dutch oven with coals on top as well as underneath. Breakfasts were equally good. For lunches we usually had cold meats, cheese, etc. and we made our own sandwiches.

A Great Place to Spend The Night   *Western River Expeditions*

On the Colorado River   *Connie Rudd*

As we continued down the river we were happy that we had decided to take the slow 8-day trip rather than the hurried one since we had the time to do so, and were able to take the side trips. We enjoyed the thrill of the rapids, the chill of being wet which was not too noticeable due largely to the thrill of being able to just drift, floating along in the calm waters without a sound. There are many streams coming from the barren land and they provided a warm and welcome bath for all. One was a waterfall so high it hurt your head to look up at it. Lying in bed at night or floating in a narrow part of a canyon, I look up at the cliffs several hundred feet high above and could not help but think what would happen if little animals pushed a rock loose up on that cliff and it had my name on it.

Just past the Nankoweap Rapids we took a side trip up to the Indian dwellings and storage sheds in the cliffs. We tend to think of the Grand Canyon as two tall cliffs, but it is not. Up from the river vertical cliffs rise several hundred cliffs, then there may be a bench or a setback of many acres before the next vertical cliff. It is on these benches that the Indians of long ago raised their corn and pumpkins, then stored them in the dry caves where it was difficult for raiding bands to steal them.

On one side trip we hiked up to a skelton on a ledge high above the river. All that is known is that the person had been Caucasian. Probably some prospector or miner who had fallen and landed on that ledge. At another location was the remains of a flimsy constucted boat which had been put together with nails. It was high above the river, probably placed there in a flood. I just wondered had someone tried to go down the river in THAT! 67

As we drifted along the color of the water changed. This was due to the Little Colorado River entering the main stream. The water is an odd whitish color because of the high concentration of chemicals. It was warm so we all had a bath there. We were warned not to drink any of the water or else we would have grave problems.

We saw many geological formations and saw the effects of past upheavals and volcanoes. We viewed the Royal Arches where swallow's mud nests hung from the ceiling. Once Crystal Rapids was not as treacherous, but a few years ago a flood came down Crystal Creek and with it many large boulders. There were lava rocks where the surrounding mountain had been washed away. On the cliffs and rocks we saw mountain sheep and many burros that were left by early prospectors and have become the scourge of the desert regions.

The ultimate rapids was the Lava Falls Rapids near the end of our trip after we visited Havasu Creek and took a shower under the falls. When you go through the Lava Falls Rapids you go through the best. The current changes frequently so before we entered it, the boatmen tied up to the bank, and went up on the rocks to watch the other boatman behind us who was a short distance upstream. He threw pieces of wood into the river. By watching the wood go through the rapids, the boatman could decide the best way to guide us through. As we went, it felt like we were completely under water, but it was only the waves and the spray. Indeed, it was a great climatic thrill.

Soon after the Lava Falls Rapids, the 'Granddaddy' of them all, we landed on the banks of the Hualapai Indian Reservation. There stood an Indian in his blue demins and black broad-brim hat to welcome us. We took a truck up to the highway where our cars were waiting. They had been driven earlier down to Peach Springs while we were on the river.

Lava Falls Rapids and Spray   *Western River Expeditions*

69

HAVASU CANYON

"The realm of the turquoise waters" - where the beauty of the land is as old as the civilization of the people that inhabit there within the environs of these multi-strated, colorful walls. The Havasupai Indians - People of the Blue-Green Waters, have lived in the Grand Canyon area for many years. Their ancestors who were here centuries ago and the descendants who are living here today add an intimate part of this ancient land.

With fresh water flowing from springs and creeks into the valley providing excellent fertile farmlands at the floor of the canyon, these Indians have been able to live here for many generations. Such magnificence and photographic beauty - the blue-green waters of the falls, and pools beneath contrast the the red Supai sandstone and Redwall Limestone canyon walls which embrace them. The upright monument rock pillars called Wigleeva, the green cottonwoods and willows with the many wildflowers along the low natural dams and creek, topped with the delicate blue sky among the summer billowy white clouds above - who would want to leave this unhurried paradise.

A cafe is the social center for the town of Supai which also has a store for general supplies, a schoolhouse, and a Mission church. There is a modern ranch style Supai Lodge with 24 rooms for overnight accommodations. Reservations are required. A campground 2.0 miles north of the village was designated by the Tribal Council for backpackers. Facilities at the campground include water, picnic tables, and pit toilets. A permit must be purchased and reservations are accepted as only a limited number of people are allowed at one time to enter and stay in the canyon. All visitors must pay a $5.00 entry fee. There is a pack train mail service as no roads go down into the canyon. No pets are allowed, nor liquor, or firearms. Now United Parcel delivers down into the valley.

Helicopter tours gently place the visitor amid the grandeur for daily or overnight stays, weather permitting. The other more strenuous entry is via the 8.0 mile trail leading from the Hualapi Hilltop down to the canyon floor reached by horseback or foot.

The trail follows along steep switchbacks on a narrow and rocky track in dry, hot desert conditions, then levels off to a plateau where the village becomes visible far below. Continuing down the Hualapai Canyon, the trail goes through deep gorges, besides bouldered streams or trickles depending on the time of year, paralleling steep cliff walls that block out the sun. After reaching the spring the green irrigated valley floor makes the walking easier to the town of Supai where stone and wooden houses are found among the meadow.

Another little used 14.0 mile approach from Topocoba Hilltop has an extremely difficult jeep-trail route from the east and south. It is believed that at one time Apaches used this trail to raid the stores of the Havasupai Indians. Later the Spanish padres used this route to get to the bottom of the canyon in search of a route to the Colorado River. The trail is not only longer, but a very poor one and unmaintained.

Havasu Falls   *N.P.S. Photo*

A jeep trail leading off the Peach Springs-Hualapai Hilltop road goes through the dusty desert out to Panya Point which offers a tremendous vista of the Havasu Canyon.

There are three main waterfalls - Navajo, Havasu, and Mooney with two other lesser falls - Supai and Beaver, as they are not as high. They all fall from the Redwall Limestone formation in such a manner as to create successive benches, and as the water falls over the edges, a series of beautiful cascades result.

NAVAJO FALLS, about a 1.5 miles downstream from Supai on the west wall of the canyon has a divided flow with a series of shorter cascades totaling 75' overall. About a half-mile further north, downstream is another varying cascade, HAVASU FALLS which pitches headlong over the western wall across from the foot of Carbonate Canyon. It is 150' high, has a divided flow falling straight on each side with the middle tumbling over shorter ridges. MOONEY FALLS, which some say is the most beautiful, has a 196' plunge of water roaring down to the pools below. The colorful, deep and narrow surrounding walls of the cliff, the luscious vegetation created by the tremendous spray, and the rain-forest setting provides a photographic delight.

Below each falls are the renown pools of turquoise. The floods and washouts that occur through various seasons, and renewed constant buildup of trapped vegetation and debris create ever-growing and ever-changing dams along the creek and at the bottom of each waterfalls that make this most unusual.

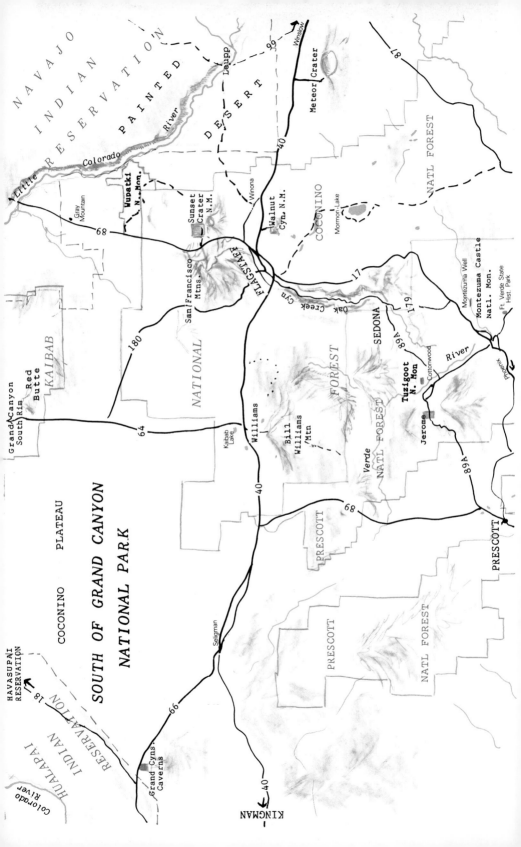

SOUTH OF GRAND CANYON
NATIONAL PARK

NAVAJO INDIAN RESERVATION

PAINTED DESERT

Colorado River

Little Colorado River

Leupp

Winslow

99

Meteor Crater

18

Gray Mountain

Wupatki N. Mon.

Sunset Crater N.M.

Winona

Walnut Cyn. N.M.

COCONINO NATL FOREST

Mormon Lake

68

FLAGSTAFF

40

San Francisco Mtns.

Oak Creek Cyn.

17

COCONINO

Montezuma Well

Montezuma Castle Natl. Mon.

Ft. Verde State Hist. Park

KAIBAB

Red Butte

Grand Canyon South Rim

180

NATIONAL FOREST

SEDONA

89A

179

Tuzigoot N. Mon.

Jerome

Cottonwood

River

Phoenix

64

Kaibab Lake

Williams

Bill Williams Mtn

FOREST

Verde NATL FOREST

89A

40

PRESCOTT

68

COCONINO PLATEAU

PRESCOTT NATL FOREST

PRESCOTT

HAVASUPAI RESERVATION

18

HUALAPAI INDIAN RESERVATION

Colorado River

66

Seligman

Grand Cyns. Caverns

40

KINGMAN

GRAND CANYON CAVERNS

It is hard to imagine when driving through the high desert plateau and grassland country on Rte. 66 that such a natural wonder lies beneath the earth's surface. These caverns with the most selenite crystals of any known cave in North America is the largest and best preserved cave system in the world.

After the forming of the Redwall Limestone layer, as seen exposed at Grand Canyon, subsequent acid water seepage through the cracks dissolved the limestone bedrock creating an underground basin. The crystalline shapes and walls of this basin were produced when the minerals of the limestone were evaporated from the acid water seepage. Through the centuries with uplifts, volcanic action and earthquakes the shape of the basin changed to form the present rooms of the cave. With the arid condition and dryness of Arizona, and the lowering of the water table as the Colorado River cut deeper, the cave became dry. Among the fossils found in the Redwall Limestone within the cave was a giant ground sloth.

In 1927, Walter Peck, a woodcutter, was surprised to find a large funnel-shaped hole that he nearly stumbled into on his way to see his friends. They all returned with ropes and lanterns to explore the big hole Walter found. They lowered a cowboy down some 150' to reach the floor of the hole. The rocks sparkled with the glow of the lantern-light and he thought he had found gold. He collected some samples to show the others. He also found the remains of two humans and an old saddle which turned out to be those of two Hualapai Indians who were buried there some time ago.

Scientists were interested in the cavemen's bones while Peck and his friends were interested in the gold. He purchased the lease rights to mine his find. He did not become rich with any gold but he did charge 25 cents for people to view the hole where the cavemen had been found.

At first only crude ladders and ropes were used for the explorations. In 1936 the government work projects constructed bridges, ladders, and stairs to make the descent possible for visitors to reach the bottom and to go along the floors of the cavern. In 1959 a newer and better shaft system was made at the present site, while the original hole found by Walter Peck was sealed. The Hualapai Indians regarded the hole a sacred place and wished it closed.

Today visitors descend 21 stories or 210' below the surface by elevator to reach the vast chambers of incredible, cool beauty with formations of breathtaking colors. The underground temperatures of 56° created by the great depth and humidity preserve the cavern's atmosphere. Well-placed lighting and paved walkways throughout the many rooms make this guided tour an enjoyable and comfortable experience. Located in the cavern building is a museum of artifacts found in the immediate vicinity. There is also a gift and curio shop.

Accommodations and services include the Caverns Inn Motel with swimming pool, riding stables, an airport, restaurant and cocktail lounges, gas station, gift and curio shops. There is a picnic area and a beautiful, clean campground situated among the juniper forest in a high desert environment near the entrance to the caverns.

Grand Canyon Cavern

WILLIAMS (6770') is snuggly situated in the ponderosa pine forest of the southern portion of the Kaibab National Forest. It is called the 'Gateway to the Grand Canyon'. All possible tourist conveniences are available with good transportation, accommodations, and services. From the Williams Airport, north of town, flights go into Grand Canyon.

Creating the spirit of the 'old frontier west', the annual events include the Bill Williams Rendezvous Days on Memorial Day Weekend, Arizona's Cowpuncher's Reunion, Old Timer's Rodeo, and Bill Williams Mountain Men Rodeo and Parade on Labor Day Weekend. The parade emulates their colorful historical forefathers in dress and customs.

South of Williams is BILL WILLIAMS MOUNTAIN (9264'), named for the trapper, guide, and mountaineer who was the first white man to explore this area. It is an all-season out-door resort area with fishing and boating in the many sparkling lakes in the summer, hiking the wilderness trails, hunting in the autumn or sledding in the Snow Play Area and skiing the popular downhill slopes or cross-country trails in the winter. At the top and end of the road is a lookout.

The Forest Service maintains campgrounds at Dogtown Reservoir (7000') from May to October. There is a nature trail, a boat launching ramp (electric boat motors only), but there is no swimming allowed. White Horse Lake also has a campground, a nature trail and boating.

North of Williams on Hwy. 64 leading to Grand Canyon are many campgrounds and resorts. On this high mesa of the Coconino Plateau the road passes through the beautiful woodlands of pinyon pines and junipers with the ground cover of grass, sage, and wildflowers in season.

At Cataract Lake (6000') and at Kaibab Lake (6800') the Forest Service maintains campgrounds among the trees with picnicking, excellent fishing and boating, but no swimming. At Kaibab Valley, the Grand Canyon Trading Post (the KOA) has tent and trailer spaces, gift shop, indoor swimming pool, market, laundry, and propane. Red Lake has a campground open during the summer months and Lone Wolf offers a souvenir shop and propane. At Valle, the junction with Hwy.180 coming north from Flagstaff there is an airport, motels, a Flintstone campground with laundry facilities, restaurant, gas station, market, curio and gift shops.

On Hwy. 180-64 a lookout point at RED BUTTE (7324') offers excellent views over the Coconino Plateau and the San Francisco Peaks. A dirt road leads east, then north about 3.0 miles where a path goes up to the top of the butte.

Above the Kaibab Limestone geologic formation at the top of the rim at Grand Canyon, the more recent built-up formations made in the Mesozoic Era has been eroded away leaving Red Butte to stand alone on the Colorado Plateau. The foundation of the San Francisco Mountain and Red Butte are made up of these later formations - Moekopi, Chinle, and Moenave, which are found at Lees Ferry and Vermilion Cliffs, and north into Bryce, Zion, and Cedar Breaks country, and east to Glen Canyon, Monument Valley, and Canyonlands National Park.

FLAGSTAFF

In 1876, in commemoration of the 100th anniversary of our nation's Independence, a scouting party placed an American flag on a peeled pine staff, which became the 'flagstaff' to the pioneers, and the name of the town surrounding it. Since that time, over 100 years later, Flagstaff has grown to be a modern community with many attractions and services. It is also the Navajo cultural and educational center. It is referred to as the 'City of Seven Wonders', as Flagstaff is the focal point for Grand Canyon, Oak Creek Canyon, San Francisco Mountains, Meteor Crater, and Walnut Canyon, Sunset Crater, and Wupatki National Monuments. The over 40,000 citizens enjoy the coolness of the 6905' elevation in the summer and living in such a magical wonderland in winter. It is the home of the Northern Arizona University, with a Symphony Orchestra, outstanding art galleries and summer festivals.

The MUSEUM OF NORTHERN ARIZONA, located at the base of the San Francisco Mountains, is internationally known for the study and exhibits of the Colorado Plateau. Founded in 1929, the beautiful stone and tile Museum features an art gallery, supports research of the Plateau area, provides instructional and educational classes, displays works of the 'Native People of the Colorado Plateau', and provides a gift shop of native American arts and crafts including Hopi basketry, pottery, and kachina dolls.

The PIONEER'S HISTORICAL MUSEUM display the life and times of the people living in the years between 1881 and 1950, with furniture, clothing, carriages, wagons, utensils, and historical photographs and other memorabilia.

In 1894 Dr. Percival Lowell founded the LOWELL OBSERVATORY where he discovered the planet Pluto in 1930. It is located on top of Mars Hill in the central part of Flagstaff. Guided tours are conducted daily at 1:30 PM. In the summer the Observatory is open on friday nights for visitors. Map making for the moon was accomplished here and today it is involved with space research in connection with NASA.

SAN FRANCISCO MOUNTAINS

The San Francisco Mountains with Humphrey's Peak (12,633') an extinct volcano, and the other three main peaks - Agazziz (12,356'), Fremont (11,964'), and Doyle (11,460') are sacred to the Navajo and Hopi Indians as the home of their yei and kachina spirits. The surrounding forest community of aspens and conifers offer a four-season paradise. With the awakening of the land from the melting winter-snow cover to the summer array of wildflowers, ferns, and birds, and the glorious display of autumn colors, this natural playground is a land to enjoy.

These peaks were named in honor of St. Francis of Assisi in 1629 with no connection to the city in California. They are part of the non-active volcanic field covering some 2200 square mile surface consisting of cinder cone, ash, and dust which includes the lava flows and the Sunset Crater to the east.

San Francisco Mountains in Autumn   *Flagstaff Chamber of Commerce*

Five life zones are in the Coconino and Kaibab National Forest areas from the floor of the Painted Desert to the top of the peaks that provide a variety of flora and fauna. The cinders that were strewed over the land at the time of the eruptions retain the necessary moisture to feed this vast area and maintain an environment to support large numbers of pronghorns, deer and elk.

There are many trails, jeep roads of dirt and cinder in the mountains that are accessible except in wet weather. A panoramic view of five states can be seen from the top of Mt. Agassiz. The Fairfield Snow Bowl is open all year with picnic facilities, snack bar at the Lodge, winter ski lifts, and summer sky rides. With the many sparkling blue lakes, bubbling springs and variants of green in the forest, fluttering golden aspen leaves, the white blanket of winter snows and the ever-changing floral display, this alpine environment entices the photographer, backpacker and all lovers of the outdoors.

Many day trips through the back roads are possible. Before venturing too far off the main roads, these back routes should be checked with the Forest Service as the conditions could vary with climatic changes. Schulz Pass Road is one of the most scenic drives between San Francisco Peaks and the Elden Mountains.

WALNUT CANYON NATIONAL MONUMENT

In 1915 the Walnut Canyon National Monument was established to protect the ancient cliff dwellings, ruins and artifacts
not previously destroyed by vandals or 'pot hunters'. In 1938
the Monument was enlarged to its present size. It is open all
year, and is about seven miles east of Flagstaff.

Under the Kaibab Limestone formation of the Walnut Canyon
the prehistoric Sinagua Indians built their dwellings as the
soft Coconino Sandstone formation below it eroded leaving caves
and sheltered ledges. The Indians closed off the front, making
partitions of adobe and stone for the various single dwellings
of one room about 80 square feet in size. Floors were made of
packed clay and the front partitions were placed back away from
the overhanging ledges to allow the rain to drip outside their
homes. There were some 200 dwellings found under the ledges and
other mound ruins in the canyon. It is estimated that about 400
to 500 people lived in this community.

The canyon is some 400' deep. They made check-dams across
the washes, used the drainage from Walnut Creek, and collected
water runoff from the rim for their drinking and irrigation of
their crops. The abundant wildlife provided food and skins for
clothing. The trees and shrubs of the surrounding slopes supplied sufficient firewood, and the native plants found in the
canyon supplemented their diet.

The Sinagua Indians made baskets and pottery for use in
their household and wove materials from raw cotton which they
grew. The jewelry they wore was made from turquoise and import-
ed shells. According to Hopi oral tradition these Indians were
their early ancestors.

A self-guiding, paved trail has been built for the visitor
to see the cliff dwellings and ruins. Many fossils
of sea animals can be seen in the Kaibab Limestone formation along the trail. A booklet is
available describing the life and the
ancient culture of the Indians.

While on the trail, in the various times of year animals that lived
at the time the Sinagua Indians lived
in this canyon, can be seen today. The
deer, pronghorn, antelope,
several kinds of squirrels,
jackrabbit and cottontail,
and a variety of birds.

The wild plants used
for food and medicine that
were plentiful along the
banks of the creek and on
slopes of the canyon also
can be seen today - Arizona
walnut, the versatile yucca
and the barberry shrub.

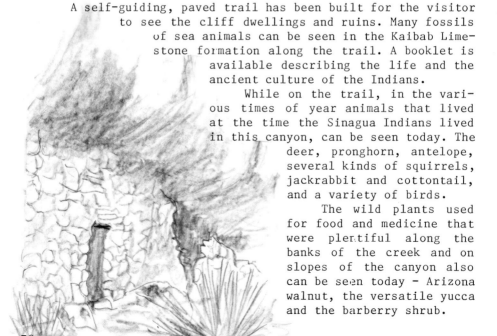

WUPATKI NATIONAL MONUMENT

N.P.S. Photo

The post-eruptive civilization of the many various Indian tribes that lived in this part of Arizona are now only wind-swept ruins on the desert mesa. At Wupatki, the largest ruin had more than 100 rooms for storage and living with ceremonial amphitheater and a ball court. Many of the walls of the pueblo ruins found here have been remortared or stabilized every few years so they will not crumble, but be preserved for future generations to observe this past generations culture. Looking out to the surrounding hills, volcanic craters, and the Painted Desert from the top of the Citadel Ruin, one can imagine the harshness of living, compared to our own, in such a beautiful, forbidding land.

Within the Wupatki National Monument of some 35,693 acres, many different tribes lived with their distinctive cultures, trading ideas and knowledge. There were two Anasazi tribes, Winslow and Kayenta, as well as the Coconino and Sinagua Indians. They settled in this fertile, rich farmlands produced by the volcanic activity to the south. Constant farming by these peoples, and the desert winds that once carried the moisture-absorbing cinder mulch and ash, later stripped the land of the volcanic soil leaving a dry and barren mesa. Gradually the Indians moved away. Some descendants of these early people are believed to live in the Hopi villages some fifty miles to north and east.

The best preserved ruin is Upper and Lower Wupatki with a circular amphitheater and ball court situated near the Monument Headquarters and Visitor Center. Over 2000 sites have been discovered within the Monument ranging from small to large, multi-roomed pueblos. The Wukoki Ruin can be reached by a half-mile road leading northeast from the Visitor Center. A shorter trail reaches the Lomaki Ruin. The Citadel Ruin, next to the Nalakihu Ruin, is yet unexcavated completely. Self-guiding pamphlets are available for trails to the Wupatki Ruin and the Citadel/Nalakihu Ruin.

The Wupatki National Monument was established in 1924 to preserve these prehistoric sites. With the close relationship of these sites to the Sunset Crater to the south, it is illustrated how land and its formation affects the lives of a civilization.

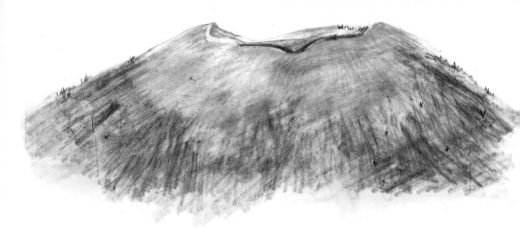

SUNSET CRATER NATIONAL MONUMENT

It was the year 1064 A.D.
The earth trembled
The sky was darkened
By a great, gray, ashy cloud.
A river of fire poured down the mountain
With steaming rocks and boulders.
Cinders fell like rain
Upon the farms and houses
And the frightened Sinagua people left.

The eruptions continued for some two hundred years. When it became known that the black cinder soil was beneficial for farming, the Indians returned to the land that trembled and settled north of the crater, which is now Wupatki National Monument.

SUNSET CRATER is the result of the most recent eruption of the San Francisco Volcanic Field. This Field also encompasses the San Francisco Peaks, some eight miles to the west. The crater is about 300' deep, and about 1000' high. The diameter at the base is one mile, and the diameter at the top is 2250' from rim to rim. The cinder cone was developed from the constant shower of ash and cinder building up during the eruption. All activity ceased around 1250 A.D. Iron oxide deposited from the vapors around the rim of the crater stained the cinders to leave the summit a glowing hue resembling a sunset. From the red color at the top, the crater cone became a soft pink, on down to the lower black portion. Because of this coloration, John W. Powell name it "Sunset Crater".

The National Monument was established in 1930 to preserve the crater from human erosion and exploitation. No climbing or hiking to the top of the crater is allowed. There is a self-guiding Lava Flow Trail which passes through the Bonito Flow in a one-mile level walk. The Monument is open all year except Christmas Day and New Years Day.

A 36-mile-loop paved road connects to the Wupatki National Monument. A campground is just west of the four-square-mile Sunset Crater National Monument. A picnic area is near the parking area for the Lava Flow Trail and Ranger Station.

METEOR CRATER

Dean Clark

When the large hole was first discovered in 1871, the initial thought was that it was an extinct volcano. However, with later findings of meteorite materials, and unusual unearth-like minerals, and with modern scientific studies, it is now known to be a crater resulting from a meteor falling to the earth some 22,000 years ago. With such a large, clean depression in the earth's surface, it is believed to have entered the earth's atmosphere at a tremendous speed. The floor of the crater is 570' deep; it is 4150' across; and the rim is three miles in circumference; and 150' above the surrounding plateau. It is the best preserved crater in the world.

At the Visitor Center there is a museum which contains artifacts and exhibits with dioramas of the area. Because of the burned-out, lifeless, moon-like qualities on the floor of the crater, the astronauts trained here before their space flights and moon walks. There are displays of space ships, the suits worn by the astronauts, and photographs of their training at the bottom of the crater. An audiovisual presentation is continously shown at the Visitor Center. Many interesting rock samples are on sale with a lapidary there to assist you. There is also a gift shop and snack bar. A small fee for the viewing of the crater from the top of the rim, and to visit the museum is charged, with a discount for senior citizens.

The importance of the meteorite phenomena and the scientific significence makes this an unusual attraction. With the modern space program and the usage of this deep, partly vertical crater for the astronaut training, it is doubly interesting, different, and educational for the young and old alike.

Daniel M. Barringer, a mining engineer, thought that the meteorite was buried so he bought the land surrounding it and for 25 years worked and studied to locate the hidden mass. In 1968 the Department of the Interior designated this area a Natural Landmark.

Lewis Clark

OAK CREEK CANYON

The beautiful, scenic Oak Creek Canyon with the white and red rocks offer the visitor all the vacation delights necessary that includes fishing, swimming, camping, picnicking, golfing, hiking, photographic excursions, and jeep tours. From the first view at the top of the rim at Vista Point looking down into the canyon and out to the valley far below, it is breathtaking. For sixteen miles the highway traverses the shores of Oak Creek down the steep-walled gorge through a veritable verdant land of flowering shrubs and cottonwoods. It is one of the most picturesque routes of all Arizona.

The spectacular panorama at the top of the canyon affords views of the switchbacks winding down into the canyon, with the distant valleys of junipers, cypress and pines sprinkled with aspens. A mingling of yellow, white, and red rocks can be seen among the dark branches of evergreens and ends with the wonderland of the buttes, domes, and red rock formations far below.

Whichever way you enter this unsurpassed and captivating stretch of highway, whether from the south out of Phoenix, or from the north out of Flagstaff, it is an ever-changing experience of color and clime.

The torrents of many spring runoffs carved a mile-wide gap between the sylvan canyon walls leaving swimming holes, fishing streams, cool picnic areas, and camping places. Rainbow and German brown trout are stocked all summer for the angler. Swimming is permitted in public pools at Grasshopper Point, Slide Rock Site, and the Sedona Community Center. The Slide Rock is a unique, natural water shoot emptying in an icy pool, a joy on a hot summer day. There are five Forest Service campgrounds and several picnic places along the creek shores.

Some of the wildlife found in Oak Creek Canyon and the red rock country are elk, deer, bear, mountain lion, bobcat, as well as the smaller animals as raccoon, beaver, porcupine, badger and skunks. There is a wide variety of birds and throughout the season the wildflowers brighten the woodland paradise.

Bell Rock   *Lewis Clark*

SEDONA

At the bottom of the canyon where the valley opens up into a more desert environment sits Sedona. This city became famous when movie directors found this grandiose setting ideal for the making of movies. At 4240' elevation, it is cool enough in the summer with beautiful trees and a charming setting to attract the attention of many artists and craftsmen. This modern 'western' city features annual art festivals and rodeos, with art galleries and unique shopping centers. The most renown is Tlaquepaque, enchanting Spanish complex named and styled after the Mexican art center near Guadalajara. The archways, cobbled walkways, and interesting architecture spread out under sycamores beneath the bell tower makes this a shoppers' paradise.

Sedona has many accommodations and services for visitors. It is the starting point for jeep tours and drives to the countryside to closely see the fantastic rock masses of spires, domes, eroded walls with carved natural arches. The Chapel of the Holy Cross and the Shrine of the Red Rocks on Table Top are favorite inspiritional structures built to capture the heart as well as the beauty of the land. The colorful rocks of white and red are enhanced by the streaks of green ponderosa and pinyon pines on the cliff sides and surrounding hills of desert lands.

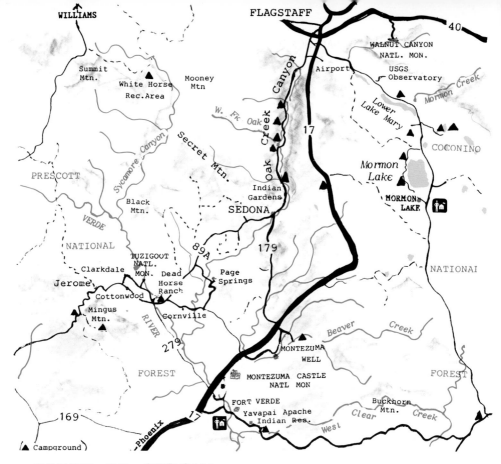

SOUTH OF SEDONA

South of Sedona are two National Monuments with three prehistoric Indian ruins that are well worth visiting: Montezuma Well, Montezuma Castle, and Tuzigoot. There are three State Parks: Jerome State Historical Park, Fort Verde State Historical Park, and Dead Horse Ranch State Park. Page Springs Fish Hatchery is also open for visitation.

For the archaeology-enthusiasts, there are other prehistoric Indian sites and ruins in this area: SACRED MOUNTAIN on Beaver Creek near Montezuma Well; CLEAR CREEK RUINS which is one of the largest Sinagua sites discovered in the Verde Valley; HONANKI with the rock paintings; and PALAKI located west of Sedona between Oak Creek and Sycamore Canyon.

In the beautiful Verde Valley en route to Jerome are two towns that were built in the late 1870's to service the miners and their families who worked and managed the mines in Jerome. Cottonwood was named for the many trees along the meandering Verde River. In Clarkdale there are many of the original homes built at that time.

North and West of Sedona is the SYCAMORE WILDERNESS AREA. It is ideal for the hiker and horseback rider as no motorized vehicles are permitted. In season, it is a favorite place to hunt quail, rabbit, deer, and elk. The Secret Mountains have some jeep roads and beautiful places to camp and picnic.

TUZIGOOT NATIONAL MONUMENT is south and west of Sedona on Hwy.89A. Tuzigoot means 'crooked water' describing the winding Verde River that flows below the ruins. Before excavation, they were completely covered with natural shrub debris, gravel, rock and sand. Hollowed out of the hill overlooking the valley and roofed with brush and poles, the box-like dwellings were constructed over five hundred years ago. They were formed around a central fortress, pyramid-type pueblo, built two-story high to accommodate the people. Many artifacts were unearthed and are in the museum. On view are bone and stone implements, bowls and pots for household use, religious clay figures, and jewelry.

JEROME STATE HISTORIC PARK is situated on the steep slopes of the Cleopatra Hill below Mingus Mountain. With quaint iron stairways, cobblestone streets, and restored buildings of the once flourishing mining community, it is an interesting ghost town to visit. Jerome once had 15,000 people living and working there. In 1953 the United Verde Branch of the Phelps Dodge Corporation closed their doors. Their copper and silver mines produced millions of dollars before the price of copper dropped in the 1930's. The population eventually went down to a mere 200.

The Mine Museum displays many important and historical memorabilia of those mining days. The popular Miner's Roost and Cafe is still open for business.

PAGE SPRINGS FISH HATCHERY is an important aspect for the fishing at Oak Creek and other streams as these trout are grown and placed in the streams for the angler. The many stages in their development can be seen in the different ponds. The Page Springs Hatchery is open daily.

DEAD HORSE RANCH STATE PARK has campsites with water and electrical hook-ups, picnic tables, and grills. Fishing holes can be found along the Verde River, and a stocked fishing pond is also in the Park.

FORT VERDE STATE HISTORICAL PARK has four original adobe buildings. They once housed the early settlers and the military personnel during the Apache wars in the late 1800's. The museum displays Apache Indian relics, military artifacts, and articles used by the early pioneers. Camping is available at Clear Creek and Beaver Creek. The Park is open all year.

YAVAPAI-APACHE VISITOR ACTIVITY CENTER is close by. It is an information center for the historical, cultural, and scenic attractions in the Verde Valley area. Slide and film programs depict the life and times of prehistoric Indians who lived in the valley and the Yavapai-Apache tribe. Museum displays are of cultural and historical significance.

East of Hwy.17 in the Coconino National Forest are streams and lakes to fish; meadows and groves to hike through; and many places to camp among the ponderosa pines and Gambel's oaks. The largest natural lake in Arizona, LAKE MORMON, was named for the early Mormon settlers who once operated a dairy there in the late 1870's. Both UPPER and LOWER LAKE MARY have camping sites near great fishing. The lakes are stocked with trout, bluegill, bass, catfish, and pike. There is winter cross-country skiing, snowmobiling, and ice fishing. The village of Mormon Lake has accommodations and services for both summer and winter.

MONTEZUMA WELL

MONTEZUMA WELL, an important geological and archaeoloical site, is an ancient civilization ruin surrounding a limestone sink fed by springs some 470' wide and 55' deep. In the encircling cliffs are pueblos of ancient Indians who lived in this fertile Beaver Creek valley. They grew beans, squash, corn, and cotton which they wove into cloth. Their diet also consisted of berries, nuts, and plants; meat from the squirrels and rabbits. They made pottery and baskets and traded with other tribes. The site is administered by Montezuma Castle National Monument.

Montezuma Well   *Lewis Clark*

MONTEZUMA CASTLE

MONTEZUMA CASTLE NATIONAL MONUMENT is one of the best preserved cliff dwellings in the United States. The cliff of beautiful whitish limestone contains apartment-type ruins that were built between the 11th to 13th century. The five-story, twenty room complex was assessible only by ladder. The Sinagua Indians grew their crops and hunted for game in the Beaver Creek Valley below the dwellings. To preserve this fragile site, no trails are permitted up to them. A self-guiding tour leads to the best possible views to admire their construction and setting. They were named for Montezuma, the famous Aztec emperor of Mexico.

The museum has a scaled model on display, and artifacts to assist the visitor in understanding the life and culture of the people who lived here. Ranger-Archaeologists are in each of the prehistoric Indian dwellings. Picnic facilities are available.

Lewis Clark

Montezuma Castle

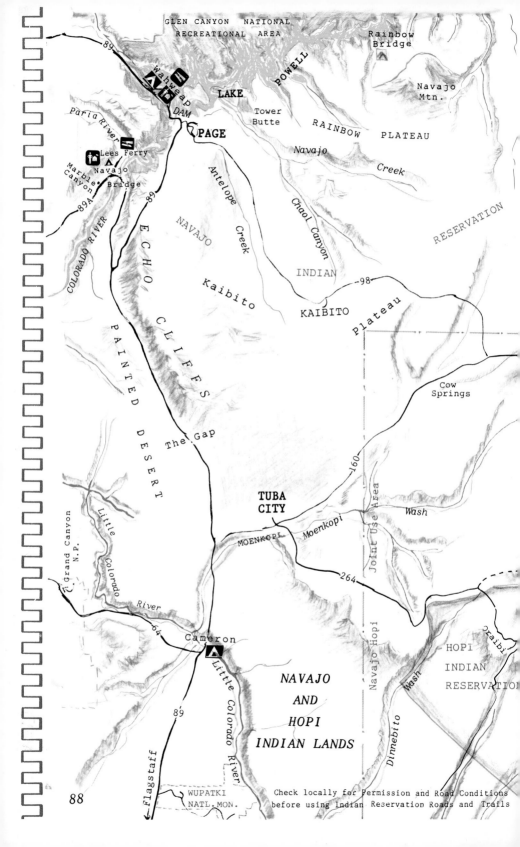

GLEN CANYON NATIONAL
RECREATIONAL AREA

Rainbow
Bridge

89

Wahweap

DAM

LAKE

POWELL

Navajo
Mtn.

Tower
Butte

RAINBOW PLATEAU

PAGE

Navajo Creek

Paria River

Antelope Creek

Chaol Canyon

RESERVATION

Lees Ferry
Navajo
Bridge

89A

89

NAVAJO

INDIAN

Marble Canyon

COLORADO RIVER

ECHO

Kaibito

98

KAIBITO Plateau

CLIFFS

PAINTED

The Gap

Cow
Springs

DESERT

160

TUBA
CITY

MOENKOPI

Moenkopi

Wash

Little Colorado

264

Joint Use Area

Grand Canyon N.P.

River

64

Navajo-Hopi

Oraibi

Cameron

HOPI
INDIAN
RESERVATION

NAVAJO
AND
HOPI
INDIAN LANDS

89

Dinnebito Wash

Little Colorado River

Flagstaff

88

WUPATKI
NATL. MON.

Check locally for Permission and Road Conditions
before using Indian Reservation Roads and Trails

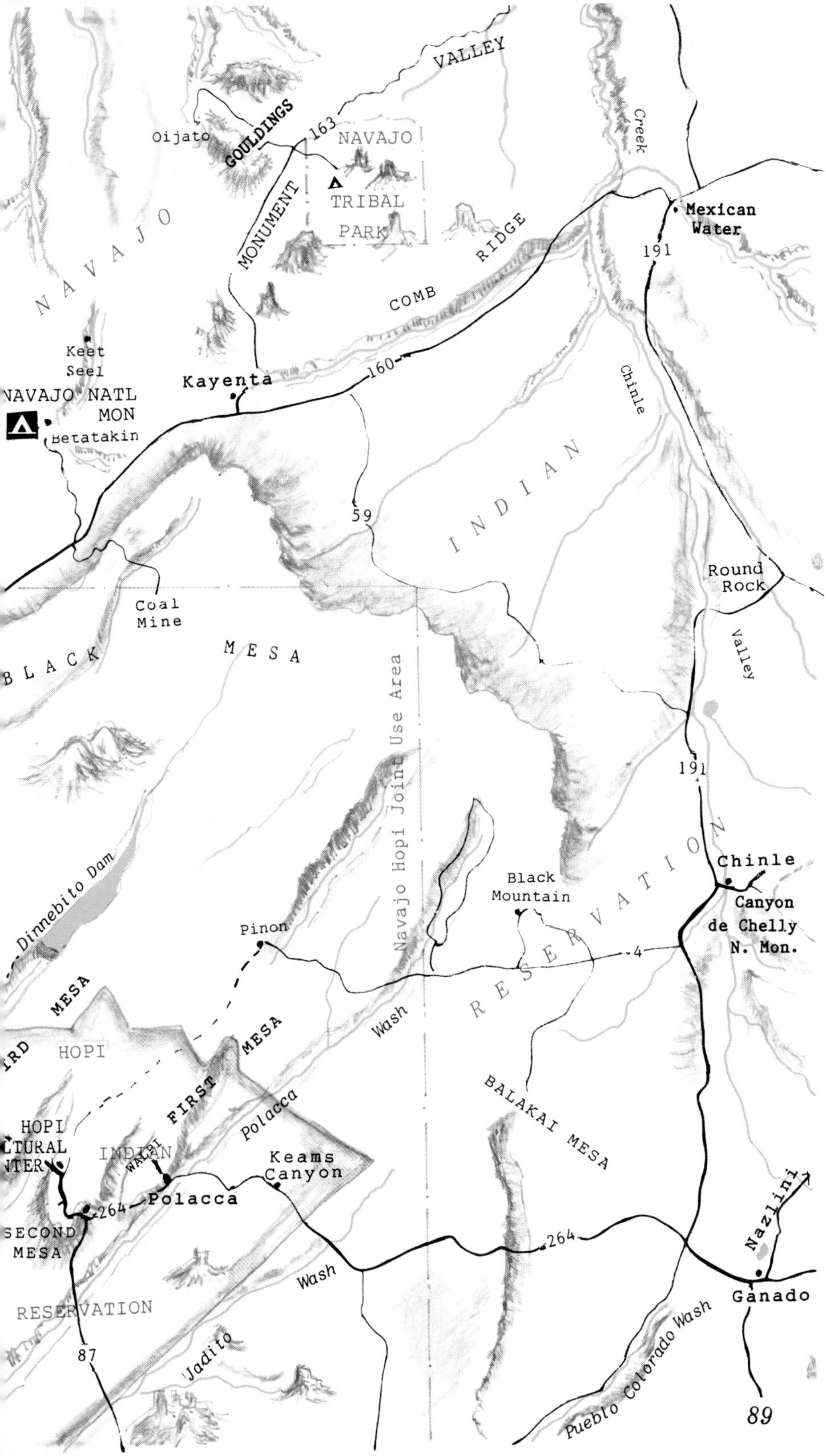

VALLEY

Oljato

GOULDINGS

163

NAVAJO

TRIBAL

PARK

MONUMENT

Creek

Mexican Water

191

NAVAJO

COMB

RIDGE

Chinle

160

Kayenta

Keet
Seel

NAVAJO NATL
MON

Betatakin

INDIAN

59

Round
Rock

Valley

BLACK

MESA

Coal
Mine

191

Navajo Hopi Joint Use Area

Chinle

Canyon
de Chelly
N. Mon.

Dinnebito Dam

Pinon

Black
Mountain

4

RESERVATION

3RD MESA

HOPI

FIRST MESA

Polacca

BALAKAI MESA

HOPI
CULTURAL
CENTER

INDIAN WELLS

Keams
Canyon

264

Polacca

Nazlini

SECOND
MESA

Wash

264

Ganado

RESERVATION

87

Jadito

Wash

Pueblo Colorado Wash

89

Hopi Gardens in Moenkopi Wash   MAC

HOPI CULTURE AND CRAFTS

The three Indian tribes living in the Grand Canyon country have three different lifestyles. The Havasupais are the river Indians as they farm the fertile fields irrigated by the Havasu Creek down by the Colorado River. The Navajos are partly semi-nomad herdsmen grazing sheep and goats. They have also become industralized with copper, coal, and uranium mining. Hopis, the pueblo Indians, live in homes on the mesa in villages raising their livestock, and farm the lands at Moenkopi. The Havasupais do not make crafts as extensively on a commercial scale as do the Navajos with their rugs and blankets, and silver and fetish jewelry, or the Hopis with their pottery, baskets, jewelry, and kachina dolls.

The Hopi Indians live on the same mesas where the Spanish explorers found them many years ago. There are three mesa areas with villages. Oraibi, on the Third Mesa, is one of the oldest continuously occupied community in the United States. Walpi, a few miles north of Polacca, is another old village on the Third Mesa built in the 1680's. Some excellent pottery is made here. At Keams Canyon, the largest community in the reservation, is the Hopi Indian Agency, Indian Hospital, and Hopi Trailer Park and campground. On the Second Mesa at Kykotsmovi are the Tribal Headquarters and Hopi Cultural Center.

They first built their homes on the mesas to protect themselves from their enemies. The Hopis are peaceful, artistic and religious people living in a comparatively small land which is surrounded by the Navajo Reservation. When the Spaniards left to return to Mexico, they gave the Hopi Indians the sheep they had brought with them. They also showed the Hopis how to grow and irrigate their crops in the washes.

Originally the Hopis wove fabric from the cotton they grew or from feathers and yucca fibers. When they realized the value of the sheep's wool for weaving, as well as for meat, they made shawls, headbands, and ceremonial apparel from the wool. The designs are usually more intricate than those of the Navajo weavers. Hopi weavers utilize diagonal twills, and a floating warp they call 'brocading'. The men of the tribe do most of the weaving.

The Hopi pottery is respected and admired as some of the best in the entire Southwest. Their work is beautifully polished, smooth, well-formed, and distinctly their own. On some pots bird symbols are painted in black and orange on white ware. The other designs used have triangular figures and curved lines. Shapes vary, being squat jars, open neck pots, low bowls, round containers, and wedding vases.

Baskets made by the Hopis are artistic, aesthetic, and as much admired as their pottery. They are quite colorful with abstract designs of birds and kachinas woven into the piece. A wicker plaiting technique is used making the baskets stiff and hard. Many mats, trays, and plaques are made in this manner. Coiled baskets are interworked with a firm foundation material, then sewn together with a more flexible fiber binding the successive coils of the basket forming the cylindrical shape.

At the Hopi Silver Craft Guild in Oraibi, exquisite silver jewelry is being made using design motifs of ancestral symbols such as clouds, corn, prayer feathers, rainfall, or kachinas. Visitors are welcome to watch the silversmiths at work. On display and for sale are pottery, baskets, kachina dolls as well as their silver work. The Guild is open all year.

At Kykotsmovi on the Second Mesa, the Hopi Cultural Center has a fine Museum and Information Center. There is also a curio shop, motel, and campground. The attractive, clean restaurant serves traditional menu selections as well as some special Hopi fare. For dinner is NokQuiVi, a Hopi stew made with Hopi corn and lamb. For breakfast blue cornmeal grits or blue flour hot cakes is offered. Blue flour is sold at the curio shop and blue cornmeal, packaged in New Mexico, is on sale at trading posts in various villages.

Throughout the year ceremonies and dances are performed. The Snake Dance, a nine-day ceremony held each year around the middle of August, is one of the most interesting of all. Some of the dances can be viewed by the general public. One year they are held at Hotevilla, on the Third Mesa, and Shongopovi, on the Second Mesa, and other years at Walpi, on the First Mesa or Mishongnovi, on the Second Mesa.

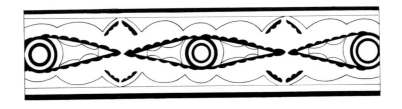

KACHINAS

Kachinas are supernatural beings believed by the Hopis to have magic power both for good and evil. These kachinas have played an important part in the life of the Hopi Indians for centuries. They are believed to live high on the San Francisco Mountains west of the reservation. These spirits are not worshiped, but are considered friends, although some are feared. Each year they come to the villages the last day of the winter solstice rites and return to the San Francisco Peaks after the Niman Kachina Dance or Home Dance in July.

Because the water supply on the Hopi mesa lands is unreliable, sometimes very scarce, the underlying stimulus for this half-year ritual is for rain. Although the most important reason for kachinas to come to the villages is to bring rain and subsequent bountiful crops, they also bring gifts for children, and the occasion for singing and dancing. There are some 250 known kachinas, and the costumes of the same kachina can differ from village to village.

The dances and the singing are by the men of the tribe who represent the various kachinas in the ceremonies. The men personify both the male and female kachinas. Each have a specific name, with a distinct characteristic or function such as Eagle Kachina, Crow Mother, Black Ogre, Clown, Runner, Great Horned Owl Kachina, or Bear Kachina.

Hopi men dress with headmasks, costumes, and/or body paint to personify a specific kachina. The masks are over-sized, made of cloth or leather, painted in bold colors with added adornments such as horns, large or small feathers, ears of corn, or twigs. Some dancers wear a ruff or collar of fox or other animal skins, roll of cotton cloth, or branches of junipers just below the headpiece. When the dancers don their costumes and perform, they lose their own identity and become that of the kachina they are representing.

Kachina dolls are made by the clansmen and given to the children during the ceremonies. From these dolls, which are replicas of the known kachina dancers, they learn to recognize and identify the many kinds of kachinas and the significance of each.

The first step in making the doll is to carve the basic shape of the figure from cottonwood roots with a knife and wood rasp. When the piece is refined with sandstone, the ears, nose, and headmask are glued on to the basic shape. Then it is completely covered with a white clay, and dried, before the final painting of bold, bright colors. The ruff and feathers, spears, rattles, and other symbols they carry are added at the end.

The hand-carved representations are sometimes very elaborate works of art, despite the fact that they are not made to be so. The craftsmanship of the Hopi men in the doll making is unsurpassed and difficult to imitate for commercial purposes. There has been some who have tried, but they are of inferior quality and cheap copies. In recent years the kachina dolls are made to show some action with dance steps, rather than just standing.

The kachina dances are open to the public, but remember, NO PICTURE TAKING OR DRAWINGS OF THE DANCERS ARE ALLOWED.

NAVAJO CULTURE AND CRAFTS

The Navajos, who originally came from northwest Canada, wandered south subsisting by hunting, gathering native plants, or raiding other tribes' crops. They did not depend on any one source to sustain themselves in any single area. In 1848, the U.S. Government wished to subdue the scavanger raiding tribe, and by 1864 they were moved to Fort Sumner, New Mexico. In 1868 a peace treaty was signed, which is still enforced today.

Returning to their homeland, they slowly reestablished a life of raising sheep and farming. Today with schools, educated leaders, irrigated farming, and the revenues from copper, coal, and uranium mining, the people are more self-sufficient. They are the largest Indian tribe in the United States with their reservation covering over 24,000 square miles in parts of New Mexico, Arizona, Colorado, and Utah.

The center and ruling member of the family is the mother. The children belong to her clan. The men own their horses, sadles, and equipment, and represent the family in public and at ceremonies. The women card and spin the wool, weave the rugs, and tend the sheep. Both men and women now do the silversmithing. The tribe is governed by the Tribal Council representing each community, who are chosen by popular vote, as is the Council Leader. The Taylor Grazing Act of 1934 limits the number of sheep and goats on the reservation and it is necessary to have a grazing permit to have livestock. Permits are passed down from one generation to another, or else bought from a permit holder.

Today there are three main religious faiths practiced: the Traditional Navajo by those who graze their sheep and believe in the Medicine Man; Christianity; and Peyote, adopted from the Comanches. Their witchcraft beliefs were acquired from the Mexicans. The Navajo people are very friendly, have a good sense of humor, enjoy the teasing of each other, and having a good time with no stress or worry.

After their return from Fort Sumner, the men learned the art of silversmithing from the Mexicans and began to make pins, bracelets, concho belts, necklaces, and other silver jewelry. They used American silver dollars until that practice became illegal, and then they used Mexican pesos. Today, sterling silver is bought by the craftsmen on the reservation in sheet form or slugs from the silver refineries. The Navajos have never mined for the silver they use. Initially they copied designs of Mexican leather work for their jewelry and rugs. As their craft developed, their own unique artistry was perfected. In 1880, Atsidi Chon started to use turquoise with his silver pieces. He felt that the blue-green stone enhanced the beauty of his silver jewelry. Today craftsmen buy the turquoise stones all cut and polished, ready for mounting. Coral and sea shell fetishes are also used along with the silver and turquoise for a variety of designs.

NAVAJO BLANKETS AND RUGS

There are twelve major districts of Navajo blanket weavers throughout the Navajo Reservation of Arizona and New Mexico. In each district they have their own distinct and specific style of design and/or color. Some type of rugs are made in all areas such as the twill or double weave for saddle blankets; reversible; or two-faced weaves. Two-face weaving has a different design on each side of the rug by laying two different wefts back to back while the reversible designs are the same, with different colors. The most common technique is the 'tapestry' weave with the changing of yarns and colors.

A variety of designs is made by using both commercial yarn and native wools with vegetal or aniline dyes. Some weavers who make a special rug use the wool from only a single sheep to ensure a uniform texture throughout the piece.

The most vivid colors of all the various rugs made by the Navajo weavers are from GANADO. They use a deep, yet warm red in quite bold effects of simple, diagonial designs with a large geometric center motif of elongated figures, and with borders of gray and black for contrasting colors.

KLAGETOH rugs, being made just south of Ganado, show the influence of their northern neighbors. Their rugs are made with vegetal dyes of red, gray, and black. Of all the blankets and rugs made in the twelve districts, these personify the most typical of this Navajo craft.

At WIDE RUINS, the characteristic patterns with bands of geometric designs are made in subtle shades of green, gold, and violet of vegetal dyes. They produce a fine weave with handspun yarn that attains a superior quality of rug. They are usually somewhat narrower in width than the more patterned blankets and rugs of the other districts.

CHINLE rugs are edge-to-edge stripes with bands of smaller geometrics separating the stripe pattern. They employ a cotton warp with duller colors of vegetal dyes for yellows, pinks, and a warm gray. These rugs are found to be more coarse than those made at Wide Ruins. A few miles south of Chinle, the rugs made at NAZLINI are quite similar with geometric stripes and bands of color in narrow widths.

At one time the CRYSTAL weavers used predominately gray or a light background color for their central design which was surrounded by a plain border. Modern weavers from this area now style their work in wavy lines separated by bands of chevrons and geometric forms. They use dark vegetal dyes as well as aniline dyes with their natural wools. Blue, rust, or reddish brown, tan, green, and yellow are the most popular colors used.

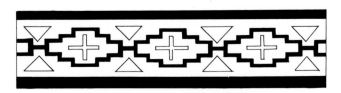

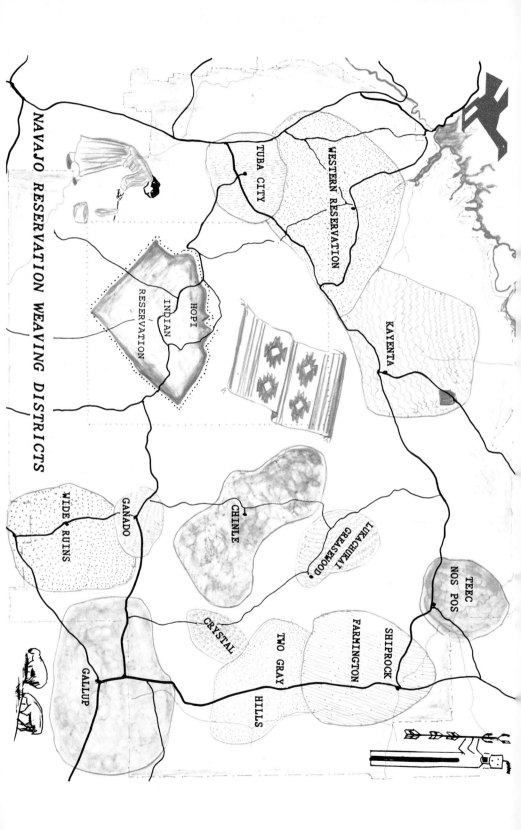

NAVAJO RESERVATION WEAVING DISTRICTS

WESTERN RESERVATION

TUBA CITY

HOPI INDIAN RESERVATION

KAYENTA

WIDE RUINS

GANADO

CHINLE

LUKACHUKAI GREASEWOOD

TEEC NOS POS

CRYSTAL

TWO GRAY HILLS

FARMINGTON

SHIPROCK

GALLUP

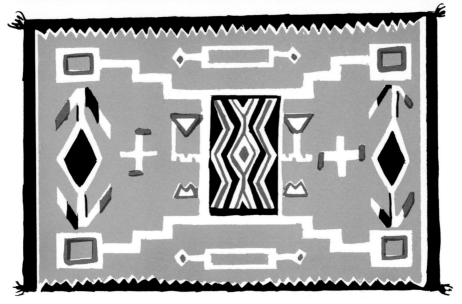

The old style Crystal rugs were the forerunners for the modern TWO GRAY HILLS weavers. They use natural colors with geometrical designs and symbols but no bands. Colors are undyed or natural black, white, or brown. For gray the black and white wools are carded together as is the brown and white wools for tan. Most Two Gray Hill weavers follow a general layout with diamonds, or stepped triangles but with their individual application, as no two rugs are alike. With the exquisite thinness of their particular close weave, these tapestries are suitable only for wall hangings and are usually smaller than those found in other areas.

TEEC NOS POS of the Four Corners area use the most complicated designs of all using many color variations with only commercial yarns. Their rugs are of forceful designs, bold, and the least typical of all Navajo rugs. Some are quite oriental in pattern. They enjoy using all available space in the design yet the rugs seem to be uncluttered and very pleasing.

The YEI or ceremonial rugs made at SHIPROCK-FARMINGTON are extremely decorative rugs with solid white or pale shades of brown and black backgrounds with tall, horizontal, geometric figures in a row, in ceremonial dress holding corn or harvest symbols. These make beautiful wall hangings. Other more modern pictorial blankets with animals, birds, butterflies, and contemporary themes are made at LUKACHUKAI or GREASEWOOD. These weavers now use bolder less classical designs.

WEST RESERVATION district covers Tuba City, The Gap, Kaibito, Shonto, and Tonalea. Their rugs are known for their storm patterns with basic rectangles and zig-zag designs of the more traditional lines symbolizing lightning emerging from a rectangle center reaching out to each of the four corners. Colors are generally gray, white, a soft red, and black.

Rugs made in KAYENTA have a white background with diamonds and borders similar to the Ganado rugs although their reds are not as rich and forceful.

SAND PAINTINGS

The sand paintings created by the Medicine Man at healing ceremonies have a deep religious connotation. The Navajos do not consider these sand paintings works of art, per se, but as an integral part of the chanting and dancing ritual performed at the time the Medicine Man is attending the sick patient. The YeiBiChi ceremonies lasts for nine days. The paintings are made on a 2" deep, smooth sand on the floor of the hogan.

The Medicine Man uses white sand and colored sands made from native sources. Charcoal produces black; cornmeal is used for yellow; minerals make green and blue; and various flowers in season for red and orange. At the end of the ceremony the entire painting is destroyed as the evil spirit causing the patient's illness is believed to be destroyed.

During this nine-day ceremony friends and relatives who have come from near and far are the guests of the sick patient and his family. They are fed and housed, and attend all of the rituals.

The deities called Yeis are depicted by long, geometrical figures holding rattles, feathers, with headdresses of corn, or small animals, or symbols of sun, moon, and stars. The four sacred colors are for the four cardinal points — white sand for the east, blue for west, yellow for south, and black for the north. The paintings are never completely enclosed by a border. An opening is left open to allow the evil spirits out and the good spirits in. This is also true to some Navajo rugs which are made by the weaver of the traditional Navajo faith. The arrangements of the square paintings are created with utter simplicity with repeated motifs.

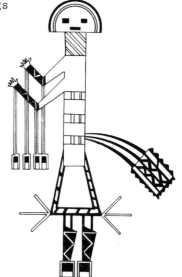

Beautiful sand painting tapestries are now made copying the figures and designs of the dry sand paintings made by the Medicine Man. They are for wall hangings as they have become exquisite works of art.

Vegetal dyes are made from roots, berries, blossoms, and seeds from native plants. From red onion skin a pale green hue can be made; an olive green from the mistletoe; a dark green from holly root and lavender from holly berries. A very pale, light green color is made from the snakeweed while the sagebrush makes yellow. Orange comes from ground lichen and an orange-pink from mountain mahogany. Other pale tones come from the scarlet creeper, globe mallow, Mormon tea, brown onion skin, gooseberry leaves, oak bark, and rabbit brush. A deep red can be obtained from the red juniper root and a good brown from walnut shells or Indian paintbrush. Tan can be made from juniper root or Dock (a wild rhubarb) root, and black from pinyon pine, ocher, or sumac.

Commercial teas are now used for beige and tan tones, or even a brownish-yellow, depending on how long the wool is submerged in the dye.

MONUMENT VALLEY
MAC

   Northeast of Kayenta, on Hwy.163, is a most colorful land
of monoliths of red sandstone towers, buttes, and unusual rock
formations isolated among the silent, solemn valley. This is in
the heart of the Navajo Nation. Many famous movies were filmed
here including "Stagecoach", "My Darling Clementine", "How The
West Was Won", and "The Legend of The Lone Ranger".

   The only accommodation within Monument Valley is the historic Harry Goulding's Trading Post and Lodge. They serve only
cafeteria-style meals at this charming old trading post. From
here daily tours are conducted into the Navajo Tribal Park and
surrounding desert lands.

   The Navajo drivers act as guides and explain the native
culture, interesting historical events, and the geological and
religious significance of the various outstanding formations.
Still living within the Navajo Tribal Park are Navajos who herd
their sheep and live as their ancestors did.

   There are two campgrounds – a KOA in Rock Door Canyon with
full hookups, tables, grills, playground, propane, hot showers,
laundry, and a general store. The Mitten View Campground within
the Navajo Tribal Park has sites that include a table, grill,
ramada, and trash containers. There is a comfort station, showers, and dump station for RV vehicles. The campground is closed
during the winter season. The Park has a picnic area and a
Visitor Center.

   Kayenta is the gateway to Monument Valley with a Holiday
Inn, motels, service stations, and stores. Many tours originate
from here with four-wheel drive vehicles to explore this magnificent red rock land. When driving on roads within the Indian
Reservation check for permission to use the road, and the condition of it. Services and accommodations are limited. Please
remember when travelling through the reservation that you are
guests. Their privacy and property should be respected. Also be
aware that the Navajo Nation observes the National Daylight
Savings Time.

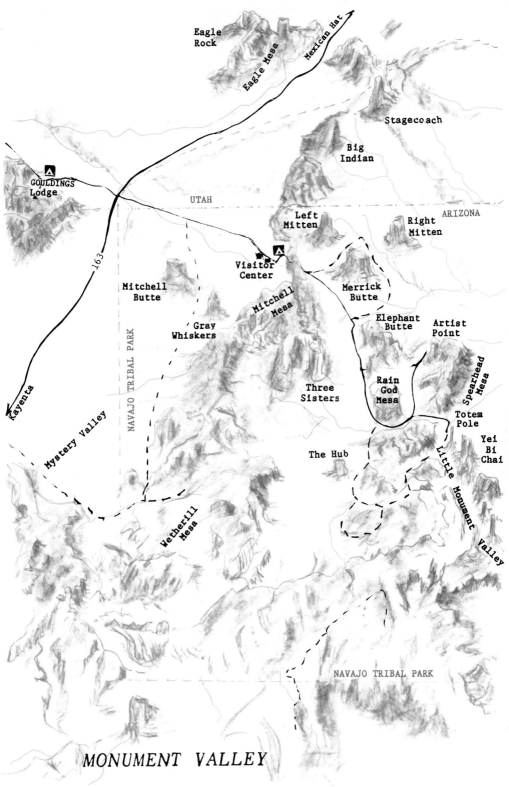

Eagle
Rock

Eagle Mesa

Mexican Hat

Stagecoach

Big
Indian

GOULDINGS
Lodge

UTAH

ARIZONA

Left
Mitten

Right
Mitten

163

Visitor
Center

Merrick
Butte

Mitchell
Butte

NAVAJO TRIBAL PARK

Mitchell
Mesa

Gray
Whiskers

Elephant
Butte

Artist
Point

Kayenta

Three
Sisters

Rain
God
Mesa

Spearhead Mesa

Totem
Pole

Mystery Valley

The Hub

Little Monument Valley

Yei
Bi
Chai

Wetherill
Mesa

NAVAJO TRIBAL PARK

MONUMENT VALLEY

NAVAJO

NATIONAL

MONUMENT

Cliff Dwellers   N.P.S. Photo

The largest and most impressive cave dwellings found in Arizona is Keet Seel, a pueblo ruins of over 700 years old. The Navajo National Monument was established in the early 1900's to preserve these ruins, as well as the equally impressive Betatakin cave dwellings nearby, and the Inscription House pueblos some miles away.

An 8.0 mile of rough trail from the Monument Headquarters leads down a thousand feet into the floor of Tsegi Canyon to reach the Keet Seel ruins. This most beautiful setting of the dwellings within the cave can be reached by foot or horseback. Visitors can explore the cave with a guide after ascending to the village by a 40' ladder. There is a daily visitation limit so reservations are required.

Betatakin, meaning 'Ledge House' is the most accessible of the ruins as it is reached by a good 1.5 mile, but strenuous trail leading from the Monument Headquarters. The dwellings can be seen from Betatakin Overlook by a half-mile footpath. From the middle of May through October there is a Ranger-guided tour down to these remarkable sheltered hillside ruins. The floor of the valley is wooded and grassy, like Keet Seel. The amphitheatre setting by the symmetrical 450-foot high arch of the red sandstone cave front towers over the huge wind-carved cavity with the two-hundred room ruins.

The Visitor Center offers exhibits and slide programs on the two ruins and a movie on the Anasazi culture. There is a picnic area and campground, where campfire programs are held. An Arts and Craft Shop specializing in Navajo jewelry and rugs is next to the Visitor Center. Remember Navajo National Monument observes the National Daylight Savings Time.

Alice Gilmore of the Arts and Crafts Shop was kind enough to give me her recipe for NAVAJO FRY BREAD: 4 cups of white flour, 1 tablespoon of salt, 2 tablespoons of baking powder, three or four cups of water. Mix all together until it becomes a biscuit dough consistency. Make a ball with the dough in your hands, then flatten it to a 6" to 8" round form. Deep fry in vegetable oil on each side to a golden brown. It can be served as bread with butter and honey or used as a tortilla for tostadas.

Betatakin Ruin

GLEN CANYON DAM

To control the flow of the Colorado River and to create needed hydroelectric power for industry and cities throughout the west, the Glen Canyon Dam was built. This dam, part of the Colorado River Storage Project, was started in 1958 and completed in 1964. At the Carl Hayden Visitor Center exhibits show the construction of the dam, and a relief model of the surrounding canyons, plateaus in the Navajo Reservation and Lake Powell. There is a self-guiding tour through the dam and powerplant that begins and ends at the Visitor Center. The modern Visitor Center was built on the rim of the canyon above the dam which enables the visitor to look down on the massive front of the dam.

The 710' gray man-made monolith which contains some five million cubic yards of concrete is 583' above the Colorado River channel and has a 1560' arched crest. There are nine generating units in the power house with a capacity of 900,000 kilowatts. Storing the water of the river in the developed Lake Powell permits controlled releases of water through the giant turbines to afford maximum usage of the drainage from the numerous surrounding canyon streams, creeks, and contributing rivers as the San Juan and Escalante. The dam and powerplant is operated by the Bureau of Reclamation and the National Park Service administers the Glen Canyon Recreational Area and conducts the campfire programs and other interpretative activities throughout the area.

The great steel-arched bridge that spans the Colorado River in front of the Glen Canyon Dam for Hwy.89 is indeed another engineering feat, as is the Navajo Bridge at Marble Canyon.

MAC

MAC

RAINBOW BRIDGE

With the curved symmetrical top and bottom forming a rainbow-shaped span, this most awesome and incredible work of the ages is aptly named. The natural bridge is 309' above Bridge Creek and the horizontal arch is 287' long. From the air this world-famous salmony-pink wonder is deeply dwafted within the rugged, colorful canyon. The slickrock, sandstone cliffs have been deteriorated through the centuries by sand-laden winds and waters. Once a sheer, narrow rock wall at the bend of a creek, the eroding away of the soft red rock left the stupendous arch hovering over the gorge and creek below.

First discovered by the archaeological expedition of Cummings-Douglas in 1909, it had been the least accessible of our National Monuments to reach. The Colorado River was some six miles down the rough canyon, and the fourteen-mile mule ride was over the arid, desert lands from the south. However, with the building of the Glen Canyon Dam it now takes a half-day or full day boat tour with an easy walk on floating pontoons from the Marina to have a close view of this magnificent span. There is a nature walk leading up to the bridge and beyond from the shore line.

LAKE POWELL

The magnificent sheer walls of red sandstone enhance the most beautiful blue-green waters of secluded inlets, scenic bays, and creeks that make up the jagged shoreline of this 186-mile-long waterway. With narrow, twisted canyons, overhanging cliffs, and unsurpassed, countless rock-walled streams entering into the lake, its awesomeness can best be appreciated by air to fully understand the full scope of the geologic display. Paved and jeep roads, and backcountry trails lead to the lake, through the Navajo Indian Reservation, and the Glen Canyon Recreational Area.

The services and resort opportunities at Lake Powell are all the visitor can wish for whether it be water skiing, scuba diving, houseboating, paddle-boating, sailboating, or enjoying an excursion cruise of either a full or half-day duration. In the cool, clear water there is swimming and diving. Fishing for large-mouth or striped bass, or rainbow trout is popular. Backpacking and hiking the trails or travelling over the dirt roads to remote places in a jeep allows the visitor to see more of the secluded canyons.

Services at Page includes motels, restaurants, stores, and an airport for scenic flights over the colorful Indian country and Lake Powell. At the John W. Powell Museum there are exhibits relating to John Powell, geology, the Colorado River, and the Indian culture. From here arrangements can be made for raft and boat trips on Lake Powell.

At Wahweap there are concession-operated boat rentals and boat tours, supplies and repairs, marina, restaurants, trailer village with full hookups, service stations, launching ramp, a large, clean campground with dump stations and telephones, picnic and fish cleaning areas, and the National Park Service Information Center. The Wahweap Campground is 4.5 miles on the paved Lakeshore Drive north of the Glen Canyon Dam with charcoal grills and tables, restrooms, and drinking water. There is swimming and diving at the Wahweap Beach near the Lodge and Marina.

Bullfrog, Halls Crossing, and Hite have a campground, airport, marina, and launching ramp. At both Bullfrog and Halls Crossing there are camping supplies available and a Trailer Village with hookups.

Touring parties are out of Wahweap by Canyon Tours, Inc. located at the Wahweap Lodge. Several day and half-day trips to the Rainbow Bridge are scheduled daily. The half-day trip takes about four and a half hours on a slick little cruiser which passes some of the most beautiful sandstone formations of domes and buttes among the numerous bays and inlets. Tower Butte, the site of the unique automobile commercial some years ago, stands out prominently.

Lake Powell and Tower Butte   MAC

THE STORY OF THE LAND

The history of the land can be read by the horizontal layers of the limestone and sandstone formations in a dramatic and colorful display of stairway geology. Descending into the Inner Canyon, passing from one stratified bed to the next, is descending two billion years in time. Each layer tells its own story of the changes that took place during the thousands of centuries which resulted in the forming of the land.

The bedrock found in the depths of the Upper, Middle, and Lower Granite Gorges of Grand Canyon at the Colorado River's elevation (2350') is the remaining basal portion of an ancient mountain range. This ancient range, from the early Proterozoic Era, is called the VISHNU GROUP. It is composed metamorphic. Originally the sandy shale blended with sandstone. The rocks were recrystalized and foliated through heat and pressure. As the centuries passed, through erosion, this hard bedrock was worn down and became exposed.

The GRAND CANYON SUPERGROUP covered the original schist bedrock. During the late Proterozoic Era great tectonic action took place lifting these sedimentary rocks and lava deposits into fault-block mountains. With the faulting, tilting, and uplifting of these layers, erosion began which in turn left only small hills and ridges of this second mountain range.

Upon the Grand Canyon Supergroup, during the Cambrian Era, the Tonto Group was deposited. The initial horizontal layer is referred to as the TAPEATS SANDSTONE. An ancient sea came from the west and slowly covered the land. The sea progressed inland and the depth of the water became greater. Near-shore deposits of reworked, coarse beach sand, deep brown in color, filled the floor of the sea. When the sea became even deeper, the waters became calmer. Deposits then included shells, dead marine life, seaweed and mud resulting in the greenish BRIGHT ANGEL SHALE formation.

Horizontal Layer Formations of Grand Canyon   *Connie Rudd*

Tonto Plateau on Bright Angel Shale Formation   *Connie Rudd*

The MUAV LIMESTONE layer, formed in the Cambrian Era, was also of marine deposits. The retreat of the sea left an unnamed layer of ripples from storms on the sea floor producing a gray crystallized calcium carbonate layer called the undifferentiated dolomites or Supra-Muav. This limestone formation is rich in shell and marine fossils as seen near Roaring Springs on the North Kaibab Trail or just above Indian Garden on the Bright Angel Trail.

The TEMPLE BUTTE LIMESTONE of the Devonian Period is a slimmer layer in size than the previous two. As the sea withdrew from the plateau, crystals and fragments of organic materials from the corals, snails, and fish were mixed with the other chemicals of the sea to form the calcium and magnesium carbonate layer of dolomite.

Upon the Temple Butte Limestone layer, during the Mississippian Period, the thick REDWALL LIMESTONE formation was built up. This impressive outstanding block of some 550' in height resulted from plankton of warm, shallow waterlands supporting invertebrate animals. This residue combines with the marine deposits of corals and shells formed the blue-gray massive hardrock. Rains washed down iron oxides from the Supai layers directly above the Redwall Limestone to stain the exposed cliffs red.

The SUPAI GROUP of the Pennsylvanian and Permian Periods resulted from the migrating sea and shore environments. Alternating layers of sandstones, shales, and limestones containing traces of iron, give the rock ledges a deep red color. The terraced formation is some 1000' in height.

The HERMIT SHALE is upon the Supai Group. It is made up of mud in which fossils of winged insects, vertebrate animals, and lush vegetation. Even cone-bearing trees have been discovered. In this deep red siltstone some worm trails have been observed. The shale formation is of a soft rock which break up and erode producing a slanting surface. A good exposure is found at Cedar Ridge on the South Kaibab Trail. The Bright Angel Trail passes through this formation after the switchbacks of the Coconino cliffs.

The tan colored COCONINO SANDSTONE was made of dunes during the Permian Period. Wind ripples and fossilized tracks can be seen in the rocks. This hard rock layer of up to 300' became vertical cliffs as erosion took place.

After the dry desert period resulting in the formation of the Coconino Sandstone layer, the sea returned. Deposits of sea shells and other marine life, mixed with mud and sand, made up the tannish-gray color of the TOROWEAP FORMATION.

The KAIBAB LIMESTONE is the youngest formation on which the pine-juniper forest of the Grand Canyon rim country lies. Most of this formation represents advancing seas. The calcium carbonate of the marine life mixed with sand, silica, and mud deposits of the sea bed formed the limestone layer of cliff rock. The deposits from the retreat of the sea have been eroded away in this area.

Differential erosion has produced the combination of the cliffs and slopes seen today. Harder limestones and sandstones become cliffs, as in the Redwall Limestone formation, and the softer shales and mudstones become slopes, as seen in the Hermit Shale formation.

Bachiopod Fossils
in Kaibab Limestone

Connie Rudd

*The eroding process of the layered formations shows   Lewis Clark
clearly in this photograph of the Green River at
Canyonlands National Park.*

More recent layers that were built up above the Kaibab Limestone formation in the Mesozoic Era have been eroded away from the Grand Canyon rim country. However, Red Butte, south of Grand Canyon, now stands alone on the Colorado Plateau. The foundation of Red Butte and San Francisco Mountains are of the Moenkopi, Chinle, and Moenave formations. These layers of rock are also exposed north of Grand Canyon National Park at Vermilion Cliffs and Lees Ferry; north at Bryce, Zion, Cedar Breaks National Parks; east to Glen Canyon Recreational Area and Lake Powell; Monument Valley; and Canyonlands National Park.

The eroding process of the layers above the Kaibab Limestone formation took many millions of years. It was not until the removal of these younger layers that the actual cutting of the Grand Canyon by the Colorado River began. At the time when the glaciers receded, the cutting away was more extreme than when the seas regressed westward.

The course of the Colorado River has always remained the same as it cut through the formations of the plateau lands. The varying width of the canyon is the result of water gnawing and gouging away the layers of rocks and fault lines through the centuries.

Inner Canyon   *Connie Rudd*

FOREST AND DESERT COMMUNITIES

Not only is the geologist intrigued with the complexities of the Grand Canyon country's environment, but the botanist and ecologist as well. In a comparatively small area most of the ecological communities are found within it – as much as those represented from Central America to central Canada. Few places in our hemisphere are more distinct with such extremes as in this region, and few places have such a wide variety of plants and animals.

These communities are a reflection of climatic belts where there is a reasonable consistency of certain trees or shrubs suitable for the shelter and food supply of its wildlife. A few general conditions that uniformly encourage animals and birds to seek a given area are:(a)adequate food supply;(b)sufficient nesting requirements;(c)specific climatic conditions necessary for their needs;(d)appropriate plant cover that provides refuge from natural enemies; and(e)special survival qualities that can provide habits such as hibernation, adaptation, and migration.

At the bottom of the Inner Canyon the dry climate and warm temperatures are similar to that of Central America and Mexico with corresponding animal and plant life indigenous to that milieu. Within the pinyon-ponderosa-juniper forest of the South Rim are the plants, animals, and birds found in a more moderate ecosystem. On the North Rim and Kaibab National Forest of the spruce and fir communities, during the winter the temperatures and environment represent the far northland and high altitudes. The ecological communities not only change in elevation within a certain area or land form, but in the angular distance from south to north as from the equator to the north pole.

No two well-established species occupy the same ecological space. Each has its own particular place for the gathering of food and for securing safety for itself and its young. The environment's amplitude determines the species and the quantity of those living there.

The natural interdependence of all living things in the Grand Canyon country, whether it be in the pine-juniper forest or the arid desert region, is constant. Not only is this true in relation to birds, insects, and animals, but it also applies to the plant communities in which they inhabit. Just as forests provide food and shelter for animals and birds, they in turn benefit the forest. For instance, the ponderosa pine tree needs the pygmy nuthatch to seek out from every nook and crevice the insects that are harmful to it. The yucca and the pronuba moth interrelate in each of their existance as the yucca plant supplies the necessary sustenance for the moth, who in turn provides the necessary fertilization for the plant. In its entirety, the wilderness residents blend like a well-run, complicated machine where each has their own part in the performance of the whole.

The interaction of all living things in the forest and desert ecological communities must be preserved. With man's presence in this wilderness ecosystem, great responsibility must be taken by him to maintain its preservation. In the canyons and desert where life is fragile, the replacement of man-made damage in some instances is never accomplished.

Pine-Juniper Forest   *Dean Clark*

ANIMALS

ELK

FOREST ANIMALS

With a good sense of smell and excellent hearing, the elk is seldom seen. Larger and taller than the deer, they can weigh up to 700 lbs. They have a dark brown shaggy mane, tan body, and a large round cream patch on the rump. Cows and calves form a herd separate from the bulls except during the rutting season. At that time the bulls engage in battles with their heavy antlers or large front hooves to determine who will dominate the 'harem'. Calves are born, one at a time, each spring, and are spotted like the fawns until late summer. Elk browse on aspen leaves, shrubs, as well as grasses of the mountain meadows. Bulls have single large-toothed antlers which they shed in early spring and promptly grow new ones back again.

KAIBAB MULE DEER

Named for the large mule-like ears, this popular animal is found on both the North and South Rims, as well as other conifer-aspen forests. Deer browse in the evening or early morning on leaves, twigs, bark and grasses obtaining some moisture from the plants they eat. They also drink at creeks and ponds. Deer are about 5' long, 3' high, and weigh about 140 lbs. As they have no upper teeth, it is necessary for them to chew cud like a cow. They have a dark red-brown coat with a black tip at the end of their 6" tail. The bucks grow antlers each year which are brown in summer, turning gray in late fall before the shedding in January or February. New growth is covered with a soft fur-like 'velvet' that protects the antlers until they become hard and sharp at maturity.

PORCUPINE

This unagressive, good-natured creature is seldom seen as he browses at night for tender shoots, buds, and leaves of shrubs and trees. He is a large, black rodent the size of a small dog. The body, rump, and tail are well supplied with stiff, sharp quills about 18"-20" long. When alarmed the quills are ejected and the barbed tips become embedded into whatever is touched. Being short-legged and clumsy with his heavy body and humped back, he shuffles from side to side as he walks. He does have bright black eyes and a large vocabulary consisting of grunts, whines, growls and chattering.

GRAY FOX

The gray fox can be identified by a slow running gate with his tail straight out. The coyote holds his down. He is the same size as a small dog, about 25" long with a 14" tail, and weighs about 10 lbs. The fox has a iron gray body with legs, stomach, and underparts a rusty yellow. There is a black stripe down the top of his bushy tail that is all black at the tip. He forages both at night and day for birds, lizards, rodents, insects, plants and berries. Coyotes, eagles, and bobcats are the natural enemies. Baby fox called 'kits' are born in the spring in dens.

COYOTE

Similar to the gray fox, the coyote is heavier and larger weighing about 25 lbs. and is 3' long. He has round eyes; long erect pointed ears and nose; and a gray body with white belly and throat. Feet, legs, and ears are a light rust color. The end of the bushy tail is dark. In Havasu Canyon the fur is thicker and healthier than average. The coyote has a keen, sharp vision necessary to catch his diet of rodents, small animals and berries. He is sneaky, cowardly and shies away from humans. If not always seen, a pack can be heard at night howling or singing.

STRIPED SKUNK

This species of skunk lives in the pine-juniper forest as well as in the thickets of mesquite or cottonwoods. Larger than the dainty spotted skunk, the size of a cat, he has a black body with a stripe of white starting at the forehead and running down over the back on each side forming a 'V' to the base of the tail. The tail is large and beautifully plumed. Scent glands are well pronounced, and the skunk can be detected often by his scent rather than actually being seen. Foraging is at dusk for squirrels, mice, rats, and insects with no fear of humans.

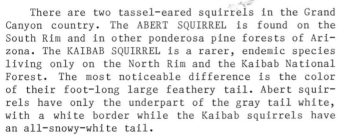

TASSEL-EARED SQUIRRELS

There are two tassel-eared squirrels in the Grand Canyon country. The ABERT SQUIRREL is found on the South Rim and in other ponderosa pine forests of Arizona. The KAIBAB SQUIRREL is a rarer, endemic species living only on the North Rim and the Kaibab National Forest. The most noticeable difference is the color of their foot-long large feathery tail. Abert squirrels have only the underpart of the gray tail white, with a white border while the Kaibab squirrels have an all-snowy-white tail.

The Abert is most beautiful with a soft gray color, tufted ears of gray on the side and a deep tawny color on the back. The Kaibab has a blue-gray body marked with brown, black belly and feet, with light colored paws. They both depend on the ponderosa pine for nourishment as they eat the inner bark, seeds, and other nuts, berries and buds found in the forest. They assist in sowing seeds for new trees as they never recover all those they so industriously bury.

Also living in the pine-juniper forest is the WHITE-FOOTED MOUSE who is a tree climber and uses abandoned bird nests for his home. He has alert bright eyes and large brown ears, short tail, a rich brown body, and as the name suggests, white feet and belly. This mouse is a nocturnal hunter for seeds to eat and to store for winter use and adapts well to various environments.

COLORADO CHIPMUNK

This distinct species is a member of the northern chipmunk family found in upper spruce-fir communities throughout the western mountains. He is about the size of the cliff chipmunk with definite bright colored stripes and gray head, crown, shoulders, and rump. He has a black spot behind and before each eye, brown side facial markings, with a sharply pointed nose. The end of the tail is dark buff. This chipmunk lives in the Kaibab Forest and on the North Rim and busily gathers nuts and seeds around the ponderosa pines.

CLIFF CHIPMUNK

This gray-colored chipmunk is a spirited fellow running and scampering among the pines and junipers. The average size is about 5" long in body and head, with a 4" dark buff tail. There is a dark line extending down the middle of the back, with less distinct stripes along the sides of the body. The stripes on the side of the face are pronounced, and lead to a sharp, pointed nose. Chipmunks usually stay on the forest floor, but will climb trees when threatened. They have a handy little pouch in each cheek for carrying food to the cache. In winter they feed from the storage piles scattered all around the forest floor, as they only partially hibernate.

GOLDEN-MANTLED GROUND SQUIRREL

This squirrel looks like an oversized, well-fed chipmunk. His personality is as colorful as the beautiful copper, yellow-gold mantle he wears. The black and white stripes on his side do not extend to the face as on the chipmunk. The ground squirrel benefits from the same shelter and food from the pine-juniper forest as the chipmunk. They share the seeds, leaves from the trees, other grasses, fruits, and berries of the forest. Being terrestrial in habit, the ground squirrel hibernates in burrows during the winter.

FOREST AND DESERT ANIMALS

BOBCAT

A skillful, resourceful nocturnal hunter is the bobcat. He is a valuable assistant in maintaining the balance of a forest or desert wherever he lives. Like a house cat, he is long-legged, weighs up to 30 lbs., has pointed ears, with tufted tips, large paws, sideburn whiskers, and a bobbed black-tipped tail. Lives in dens found in hollow trees or rocky crevices and caves. He hunts for birds, squirrels, and rodents on the ground, suns himself on warm rocks or boulders, and when in danger climbs trees. Kittens are born in the spring and are carefully protected by the mother. Tracks of the bobcat found in winter snows verify his existance as he is seldom seen.

MOUNTAIN LION / COUGAR / PUMA

This magnificent animal is found in the same area as the mule deer. Being a meat eater, he also catches skunks, porcupines, squirrels, mice and rodents. Very silently he creeps along on his belly when hunting, and then lunges for the catch. The lion is powerful, yet timid and well-mannered. The beautiful soft sandy colored coat hangs loosely about him for flexibility, adapts well to the rock or desert background of the surroundings. With a slender build; long tail; strong jaws; and large paws, he is a good climber and jumper. A menancing, deep growl can be heard if near, although is seldom seen.

BIGHORN SHEEP

The sheep, found in rugged, remote canyon slopes and isolated desert regions of the Grand Canyon country, are smaller than the California Sierra Nevada bighorns. The tannish-buff color adapts well to the environment but the light colored, almost white patch on the rump can be spotted from afar. They graze on shrubs and greases, thistles, and other flowers traveling in bands of three to ten with ewes separately from the rams. For their size, they are quite agile as they leap and jump over the rocky terrain effortlessly. Unlike deer or elk, the bighorn sheep never shed their horns. Age is determined by growth rings. The horns of the rams are massive, round, curving to half circles, some weighing up to 40 lbs., while the horns of the ewes are flat and erect.

STRICTLY DESERT AND OPEN RANGE ANIMALS

PRONGHORN ANTELOPE

These graceful, intelligent members of the antelope family are timid, enjoy the open range, and live on sagebrush flats, usually in a group, feeding on grasses or desert plants. They are built for speed. With a smooth, level, sprinted gait, they seem to delight in running. They are reputed to be one of the fastest North American mammals. Their sensitive nose and bright large black sharp eyes can detect small motion even from far away. The ability to outrun any enemy is their security.

The beautiful creatures have distinct horns which rise from the skull above the face. Every fall the horns are shed and each spring new ones grow over the remaining cores. The horns on the female are smaller than those of the male. The soft, buff color of the body contrasts with the white markings on the rump, side of head, belly, and breast. Two front bands are on the throat and patches on top of the nose and under each ear. The white rump patch is of stiff, long hairs, and projects when the antelope is frightened.

BADGER

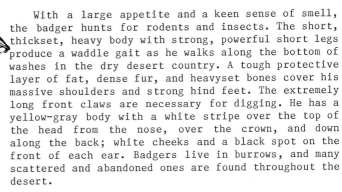

With a large appetite and a keen sense of smell, the badger hunts for rodents and insects. The short, thickset, heavy body with strong, powerful short legs produce a waddle gait as he walks along the bottom of washes in the dry desert country. A tough protective layer of fat, dense fur, and heavyset bones cover his massive shoulders and strong hind feet. The extremely long front claws are necessary for digging. He has a yellow-gray body with a white stripe over the top of the head from the nose, over the crown, and down along the back; white cheeks and a black spot on the front of each ear. Badgers live in burrows, and many scattered and abandoned ones are found throughout the desert.

RINGTAIL CAT

A shy, timid, gentle, yet agile and alert little mammal of the raccoon family that was the pet of the miners. Fox-like appearance, he has a sharp pointed snout; large ears; a broad head with bright dark eyes that enable him to see in darkness. The eyes are encircled with a white ring and between the eyes there is a black spot. Its' light-brown-gray fur is short and smooth. Seven black and white furry bands characterize the tail that is graceful and bushy. The tail, being as long as the body, helps him to quickly scamper over rocky ground and piles, in and out of rimrock caves and crevices where he lives. When cold, the ringtail cat can curl up into a furry ball with his tail and keep warm. He is active at night hunting for mice, lizards, birds, insects, fruit and berries.

SPOTTED SKUNK

This sprite night hunter is smaller in size than the striped skunk. Known in the fur-trading days as the 'civet cat', he is actually neither. The dens are made in burrows among rocky hillside canyons or in brushy desert country. He has broken white lines, or spots on his glossy, dense, smooth black body; long black front paws for digging; and a black tail with a white tip. The diet consists of plants, eggs, insects and mice. In turn, he is hunted by the mountain lion, eagle, and the great horned owl.

BLACK-TAILED JACKRABBIT

A true hare, the jackrabbit can outrun a dog and leap up to 20'. He is basically a pale gray color with a yellow tinge, has a white belly and a black streak on top of the tail and rump. The large ears - 6" to 7" long, are tipped with black, and through special openings, the jackrabbit is able to lose the excess body heat. He drinks no water but receives the necessary moisture from the grasses, leaves, and bark of the desert plants he eats. With very strong hind legs, sharp eyes and hearing, he can rely on speed for safety. He is born with fur; eyes already open; and can hop. Living in the open desert, he forages in the early morning or evening and hold up under bushes in cool burrows called 'forms' during the heat of the day.

DESERT COTTONTAIL

The cottontail is a true rabbit, being smaller, daintier and more compact in body than the hare or jackrabbit. He also has a light gray coat tinged with yellow. The tail is short, white and fluffy, and the ears are only 3" to 4" long. He lives in thickets, needing the heavy brush cover to hide him from predators and seeks shelter in burrows or rock crevices from the hot sun. Both night and day he feeds on the desert grasses and plants from which he receives all necessary moisture. The eyes of the rabbit are closed when born; have no fur; and is helpless for at least a week after birth.

ROCK SQUIRREL

The rock squirrel lives and forages for vegetation in the open desert and nests under boulders. He enjoys surveying the surrounding country while sitting upon rocks and boulders. This rodent is the largest species of ground squirrel, being 12" long, with a 10" tail. He wears a gray-brown coat and hibernates in the winter.

WHITE-TAILED ANTELOPE SQUIRREL

A desert ground squirrel common in the Grand Canyon country is the white-tailed antelope squirrel with a single white line on each side of the mostly pinkish-gray body. With a 2"-3" tail curled up and over the back, the little white fur of the undersurface resembles the white rump patch of an antelope.

There are many small rodents that live in the rocky cliffs, open desert or canyons. The DESERT WOOD PACKRAT lives in low cactus-covered regions collecting metallic objects, bright wrappings or whatever he can scrounge. He piles desert debris and spines in front of his little cactus den to keep the treasures. The wood rat is gray and tawny colored with a hairy tail almost as long as his body.

THE KANGAROO RAT, a dainty little desert dweller obtains his necessary moisture from dry grasses he eats by a special metabolism. The ROCK POCKET MOUSE belongs to the same family as the kangaroo rat and eats dry plants and lives without water. The little gray colored mouse has cheeks with a fur-lined pouch that allows him to carry seeds and food back to his nest. He has small ears and a long tufted tail.

The buff colored CANYON MOUSE has white on his belly and the undersides of his long hairy tail, which ends in a slight tuft. The CACTUS MOUSE has no tuft at the end of his tail, and large ears. In the cool of the night he scurries about hunting for his food.

BIRDS

During the course of a year through various migrations, a number of birds are seen in the deserts, canyons, forests, and grasslands along the Colorado River and its tributaries. Within this sphere the birds are identified scientificially into species and subspecies and by characteristics, habits, or method of feeding. The different types of birdlife are creepers, birds of prey, perchers, singers, flycatchers, game and water foul.

Flycatchers such as the phoebe, pewee, swallow, or swift feed on insects caught on the wing with their trap-like beaks. Other birds with sharp, curved beaks bent like a hook as the falcon and hawk, seize and tear the flesh of dead animals or of its prey. Seed-eaters as the junco or grosbeck have a short, thick bill that is strong enough for crushing. Chickadee, titmouse, and nuthatch have slender curved bills which probe cavities of trees and bushes as they creep along searching for insects. Bills on the wren are thin; thick on the sparrow, and long for the belted kingfisher, efficiently used as a scoop for food.

The woodpecker bores into and around the bark beneficially killing beetles and insects that destroy trees. Birds such as the sparrow or jay feed on the ground hopping about, while the warbler rummages through dry leaves. The breasts of birds can be plain, spotted, or streaked. And, of course, the passerine birds like the robin, bluebird, and vireo are identified by their various cheery or squawking noise in the forest, meadows, and canyons.

Some birds have a long tail as on the swallow; medium as on the robin; and short as on the meadowlark, while others hold the tail up in a perky fashion like the wren and water ouzel, or down like the raven and flycatcher. Flying habits differ; some soar like a hawk or skim the air like the swallow, hover like a hummingbird, or go straight like a dove. Tail shapes are either notched W like the swift or finch, square like cliff swallows and some warblers, round like the jay or cardinal, pointed like the dove and falcon, or forked like the barn swallow.

Generally the nest is not a home for birds as it is only a safe bedding place for the young. Other birds or small animals like mice take over abandoned nests. Birds are seen primarily in the spring, summer, or autumn, although there are year-round residents such as the raven and pygmy nuthatch. The male of each species is the most striking member; females are usually less vibrant in color to be less noticeable while nesting.

There are a number of water foul and game birds that make their seasonal home in the Kaibab Forest, along the Colorado River and large streams, and in the surrounding canyons. From Canada and the Arctic tundra northland the geese, ducks, teals, mergensen and coots visit in the autumn. The eared grebe is quite common as is the large stately blue heron which feeds on fish or small animals found in the nearby desert. The cinnamon amd green-winged teals are commonly seen, as are the mallard, pin-tail duck, black-bellied plover, and spotted sandpiper. Another common migrant is the beautiful shoveller with its long spoon beak and neck and head of dark green with brown sides and white breast, red belly and sides. The Canadian and blue snow goose, though once common are seen only rarely now. The kildeer who is a member of the plover family, is found in fields as well as along the river banks or shores of streams. The pin-tailed duck has a graceful neck, with a white breast and belly that extends down to the tail which gives him a sleek elongated appearance. He seems to rest atop the water rather than dive down into it as do other species of ducks.

CACTUS WREN   SONGBIRD
(Heleodytes brunneicapillus)
Has a spotted reddish breast, about 8" long, and is the largest of the wrens. White streak over the eyes and white markings on the tail feathers. Eats insects. Jerks his tail as he perches on yucca and cactus. Nests in mesquite, cholla cactus, and other thorny bushes.

CANYON WREN   SONGBIRD
(Catherpes mexicanus)

This little wren is about 5" long, with a long curved beak. Has a white throat and dark red-brown belly. Found along the Bright Angel Trail and other brush and rocky places. Builds nest in streams among rocks. Darts in and out of canyons.

ROCK WREN   SONGBIRD
(Salpinctes obsoletus)
Frequently seen in the Kaibab National Forest and the North Rim during the summer. Has a brownish-gray body with a finely streaked breast, white streak over the eye and a tan tip on the tail. Is 16" long. Darts in and out of rocky slopes and canyons. Has a rather harsh song. Builds nest among grasses.

WESTERN BLUEBIRD   SONGBIRD
(Sialia mexicana)

The head, tail, and wings are all blue with back and breast a reddish color. The bluebird is frequently seen in the pine forest. Has a slender bill, is about 7" long with a 3" tail and long legs. Eats insects and berries of the mistletoe. Female has brown body coloration with tail and wings blue. Belongs to the thrush species, as is the robin, for the young are speckle-breasted. Spends considerable time perching on tree tops.

121

YELLOW-BREASTED CHAT   SONGBIRD
(Icteria virens)
    Has olive-brown, throat and breast yellow, and
white belly. The eyelids and stripes over the eye are
white. Is about 7" long with long 3½" tail. A very
secretive bird, found in bushes, briars and thickets.
A most vocal warbler imitating other bird songs. Has
slow movements, yet can be active in a playful sense.

WESTERN TANAGER   SONGBIRD
(Piranga ludoviciana)
    The flight in and out of sunlight and shadow of
the tanager is a thing of startling beauty. Has vivid
scarlet head, upper back and tail black, wings black
with yellow bars, the rest of body a striking yellow.
Movements are slow and deliberate. Female has a dull
green and yellow underparts with white wing markings.
Eats berries and insects. Common in the pine forest.
Sings happily like a robin.

BLACK-THROATED GRAY WARBLER   SONGBIRD
(Dendroica nigrescens)
    The black and white stripes on the gray face and
black throat are distinctive. Is only 5" long, and
smaller than a junco. Has a short bluish-gray tail
with broad white edgings. The female has a dull green
body and yellow underparts also with the white wing
markings. Eats berries and insects. Commonly seen in
pine forests. Sings happily like a robin.

PYGMY NUTHATCH   CREEPER
(Sitta pygmaea)
    Found in the Grand Canyon country in the pine and
juniper forest. Creeps and feeds with a long bill to
pick out insects found in the barks of the pines. Is
4½" long and smaller than the white or red-breasted
nuthatch. Feeds facing downward on tree trunks. Has a
short stubby tail, head capped with a gray-brown color down to the eyes. Underparts are a pale tannish
yellow. When in flight the entire flock chatters in a
harsh twitter. Other creepers are the chickadee and
titmouse.

MOUNTAIN CHICKADEE   CREEPER
(Parus Gambeli)
    In small groups the little chickadees searches in
foliage and twigs of conifers for insects, larvae or
spiders. They creep along, sometimes upside down, on
the bark, and rarely on the ground. Smaller than the
junco and sparrow, lives in the forest all year round
enduring the cold snowy winters. Their thick, soft
feathers protects them. Has persistent identifying
call 'ee-chee-chee'. Nests on tops of trees. Top of
head and throat dark, white line over eye, cheeks and
breast white, slender curved probing bill.

PHAINOPEPLA
(Phainopepla nitens)
FLYCATCHERS

Called the 'Silky Flysnapper' in early pioneer days in the Southwest because of his sleek black body and catching insects on the wing. About the size of an oriole, 8" long, with a distinctive broad white patches on the wing, and a slender long crest with loose feathers. Female is a dull dark gray color with no white patches. Found in the desert areas among the mesquite trees. Has a soft, weak, disconnected song.

VIOLET-GREEN SWALLOW
(Tachycineta thalassina lepida)
FLYCATCHERS

This beautiful passerine-percher has a green and purple back, bronze head, purple rump, white underneath and side of neck. With a small body, about 5½" long, full wings for a graceful flight, and very weak feet. Soars above the ponderosa pines or in and out of canyon walls. Feeds on insects caught on the wing like the swift. The two white patches at the base of the forked tail distinguishes this bird from the tree swallow. The CLIFF SWALLOW has a square tail and a dark throat with a light buff rump.

WHITE-THROATED SWIFT
(Aëronautes saxatalis)
FLYCATCHERS

Often confused with the violet-green swallow, the swift is actually related to the hummingbird. Found in similar canyons, it can be identified by the white markings on the breast and throat. Has long, narrow wings which are kept stiff when in flight, long and slighted forked tail, and a dark brown crown. Nests in the canyon cliffs and crevices. With rapid wing strokes, the swift darts, and plunges, turns, and twists as he sails with wings slightly downward.

WATER OUZEL
(Cinclus mexicanus)
DIPPER

This bird loves to move up and down with quick movements darting in shallow streams around the bottom rocks seeking his food. Walks under the water and is able to use wings for propellers. Is about 7"-8" long, with a short tail that is held upward, and has white around the eyes. Looks somewhat like a chubby wren with a slate-gray coat. The clear "seet" song, repeated, is heard throughout the year.

YELLOW-BELLIED SAPSUCKER
(Sphyrapicus varius)
WOODPECKER FAMILY

Also called the Red-breasted Sapsucker as the head and breast are red and is sometimes mistaken for a red-breasted woodpecker. As the name implies, has a yellow belly with back and wings black with white markings. This bird bores rows of holes around the trunk of the tree in an orderly fashion and sucks out the sap as it oozes out of the openings. Also eats the cambium. Found among cottonwoods, willows, and aspens. A shy bird with a soft, squeal sound.

PINYON JAY
CROW FAMILY
(Gymnorhinus cyanocephala)

Seen and heard in flocks in sagebrush country and in the pine-juniper forests, the pinyon jay struts about feeding on insects and nuts from the pinyons. About the size of a robin, 11" long, has a dull blue coat and lighter, almost white markings on the throat with a short tail and a straight sharp bill. This jay does not have a crest as the stellar jay. Is as noisy as the stellar jay but not as raucous or harsh.

CLARK'S NUTCRACKER
CROW FAMILY
(Nucifraga columbiana)

With a noisy, grating cry, this crow family member is the size of a blue jay, 13" long, with similar companionable habits. Has pale gray body with dark wings, dark center on the tail and outer edges of feathers, with the rear of wings white. Feeds on insects and pine nuts which are pried out of cones, as the pinyon jay, with a long, pointed bill. Found in high rocky places.

RAVEN
CROW FAMILY
(Corvus corax)

The raven is twice the size of the crow, about 15" in length. Sometimes it is hard to differentiate the two. With a noticeable wedge-shaped, full tail, a glossy black body and wings with a purple overtone, black bill and feet. The long pointed wings stay horizontal when in flight as they soar in warm thermals of rising air. When walking on the ground, the raven has a hop and strut. Usually seen alone, but will gather at a carcass, as the diet is usually dead animals. Has a rather harsh croak, while the crow has a caw sound. Nests in twigs on cliffs and trees in the desert regions.

WESTERN MOURNING DOVE
DOVE
(Zenaida macroura)

The distinct plaintive, mourning "caah-cooing" of the male dove is found throughout the west. With a soft brown body and pinkish chest, somewhat like a pigeon, as this wild dove belongs to the pigeon family. Measures about a foot in length with a pointed tail with white markings that can be seen clearly when in flight. Likes to drink water in the morning and evenings. Perches in the mesa, fields, on bushes and trees. Feeds on seeds of the thistle poppy and amaranth found on the ground.

BELTED KINGFISHER
NON-PASSERINE
(Megaceryle alcyon)

The kingfisher flies over the river and along the creeks seeking out fish to scoop up with his long 3" stout bill. The ragged, bushy crest on his blue-gray head rises when perching. Has a marked white breast with blue bands and a white collar around the neck. The female has two breast bands. About the size of a dove - 12"-14" long. Has a chattering cry.

124

GAMBEL'S QUAIL
(Lophortyx Gambeli)
TERRESTRIAL

This is the desert cousin to the California Quail found in the Sierra Nevada. Shelter and food are supplied by the mesquite tree and hackberry bushes. The nests are on the ground under bushes lined with twigs and leaves. Diet consists of greens and fruit, with succulent plants providing the necessary water. Has a drooping head and a single curved plume. Male has a large black spot on the tan belly with a red-brown patch on the head, with a matching color on the wings which contrast the gray body. Being terrestrial, it is a strong runner and can scamper rapidly from prey. Coveys communicate in low, soft tones as they call or sing.

ROAD RUNNER
(Geococcyx californianus)
TERRESTRIAL

Also known as the 'Chaparral Cock', this unusual bird can be seen running along the desert ground or the roadside with the long, narrow tail straight up, measuring about 22" long. Feeds on insects, lizards, or snakes. With a black shaggy crest, white belly, heavily streaked brown body, and rounded wings. The strong legs enables him to glide or fly close above the ground. Eyes have a blue-gray patch behind them. Nests are found in low trees or cactus made up of grasses and sticks found in the desert.

DESERT SPARROW HAWK - AMERICAN KESTRAL
(Falco sparverius)
BIRD OF PREY

The kestral is a member of the falcon family, the only member with a reddish tail. It is one of the most colorful birds with a red-brown crown, back and tail. Slightly larger than the robin, about 9" long, has long, narrow, pointed tail with a black band near the tip, wingspan is about 2', gray-blue coloration on the wings, and yellow feet. Flutters and hovers, moving wings rapidly while head is bent forward, then quickly dives to a pinpoint landing on the prey of insects, mice, lizards, and grasshoppers. Likes open country but nests in cliffs or in holes of trees or poles.

TURKEY VULTURE or BUZZARD
(Cathartes aura)
BIRD OF PREY

Found in the desert, rocky places or along wooded streams and brush. It is a soaring bird that glides in a wide circle without flapping the 6' wings looking for dead animals. The black body is contrasted by the small, bald, red head. Similar to the eagle and hawk, the wings have a silver-gray underside and the upperside brownish-black. Spreads the feathers at the tip of the wings like fingers to capture all possible air currents. Common in the Kaibab National Forest in the summer.

FLOWERS AND SHRUBS

WILD ONION   LILY FAMILY
(Allium palmeri)

A perennial plant that grows from bulbs with the taste and smell of onions, found in brushy and woody places. The flowers are delicately striped in purple, pink or white in an umbrella-like cluster at the end of a stout leafless stalk. Blossoms have three sepals and three petals with six stamens. The two narrow, flat leaves grow at the base of the flower stalk. The bulbs are used for food and flavoring. Golden-mantled ground squirrels eat the wild onion found on the South Rim in the pinyon-juniper forest.

LOUSEWORT/WOOD-BETONY   SNAPDRAGON FAMILY
(Pedicularis centranthera)

The fern-like leaves grow in a rosette cluster close to the ground. Leaves are toothed and tipped with white. Blossoms are white and lavender bunched close together on a short spike. They are two-lipped: the upper lip is hood-shaped with the tips of stamens protruding down looking like teeth; the lower lip is three-lobed with the two outer being larger than the middle. Found on both rims of the Grand Canyon in the pinyon-juniper forest.

LATE SPRING, EARLY SUMMER

MORMON TEA   JOINTFIR FAMILY
(Ephedraceae)

The slender, many-branched, jointed, gray-green stems have two or three scale-like leaves at widely separated nodes. The central trunk is thick and shaggy. Male and female species are on different plants, but grow close together in a colony. White flowers of the female have seed bearing, scaly, light brown cones at the leaf nodes containing two seeds each. The male flower carries yellow-brown pollen-bearing cones.

Also referred to as squaw, miners, Brigham, or Mexican tea as pioneers and travelers steeped the dry or green twigs in boiling water for a beverage. The plant is known to have medicinal benefits. Navajo Indians make a light brown dye for their yarns from the plant. Animals eat the seeds, and bighorn sheep and deer browse for the foliage.

CLIFF ROSE   ROSE FAMILY
(Cowania mexicana stansburiana)

The creamy-white, yellow-centered rose is a branched shrub about 8'-10' high with dark twisted bark and reddish-brown twigs. Leaves are green above with densely matted white hairs beneath; 3-5-divided segments; hard and small. In the autumn the fruit has five seeds each with 2" long, white, feathery tassel. The coarse matted, rough bark was used medicinally by the early Indians and is used by the Hopis today. It grows on slopes and mesas, along the road in the pine and juniper forest. Seen on both the North and South Rims.

ROCK-CRESS   MUSTARD FAMILY
(Arabis pulchra)

    A purple-pink flower with six stamens and four
petals found on rocky slopes and in the pine-juniper
forest. The alternating, about 3" long, bluish leaves
are more numerous at the base of the plant. Flowers
grow at the top of the single or branched stems.
Sepals are erect, oblong and uniformed. The seed pods
are straight, flat and long, hanging down. Seeds are
many, flat, oblong and winged. Pods and leaves are
covered with a fine hair.

                      SQUAW BUSH   SUMAC FAMILY
                      (Rhus trilobata)
        This pale yellow flowered, deciduous shrub found
in canyons, washes, and the pine-juniper forest is
often confused with poison oak. The squaw bush has no
allergic producing properties, however. The 5-petal
flowers are in clustered spikes that appear before
leaves. Three main shiny, 3-lobed leaflets are alternate leaves that have a strong odor when crushed. In
the fall leaves become a striking red color. Berries
are hairy, flat, sticky, and reddish. The animals and
birds eat them. Indians make dye from the plant and
use the berries as fruit or ground into flour.

DESERT PLUME/PRINCE'S PLUME   MUSTARD FAMILY
(Stanleya pinnata)

    Found in the semi-desert, dry mesas along with
sagebrush and pinyon pines, the yellow flower spikes
are on top of the tall woody stalks. The buds at the
top of the stalk develop as the plant matures. The
flowers have four petals with hairy claws at the base
and four sepals. Fruits are 1"-3" long pods
extending alternately from the stem. Leaves are also
alternate, long and narrow, and pale green. Indians
used the plant for herbs and seeds were ground for a
mush. Quite common at Wupatki National Monument.

                      FERN BUSH/DESERT SWEET   ROSE FAMILY
                      (Chamaebatiaria millefolium)
        Found in the pinyon-juniper forest, this beauti-
ful, aromatic plant has white petals with yellow centers is similar to a small wild rose. It grows in
abundant flowered clusters on top of erect branches.
The 3'-5' branches are several stemmed and reddish
in color. The fern-like leaves are alternating, scaly
and sticky. Seen at Yavapai Point on the South Rim
and at Walnut Canyon National Monument.

COMMON MULLEIN   FIGWORT FAMILY
(Verbascum Thapsus)

    First introduced from Eurasis, this common field
and roadside wood plant is found throughout the west.
The small yellow flower blooms on a long, 3' dense,
terminal spike. The stout unbranched stem, from 3'-6'
high is erect. The yellow flowers produce brown seeds
and at one time the tall, dried stalks were dipped in
grease and used as candles or wicks. Leaves are
alternate, forming a wooly, gray-green rosette at the
base of the plant. Indians used the plant for medicinal purposes. It is not a favored plant now although
it was an Old World herb with many beneficial uses.

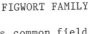

YELLOW MONKEYFLOWER   FIGWORT FAMILY
(Mimulus guttatus)

Deep in the Inner Canyon all through the summer this foot high perennial can be seen. At the top of the stem is the two-lipped yellow flower. The term of 'monkey' refers to the face-like appearance of the blossom. The leaves are opposite, about an inch long, delicate, tapered, and toothed. The Indians used the young stems and leaves for greens and the root was an astringent.

The crimson monkey-flower *(Mimulus cardinalis)* grows up to 4' high and is found along streams in the shady canyons and near waterfalls. The scarlet flower is about 2" long with the tube being longer than the limb. It resembles a snapdragon.

PENSTEMON / BEARD TONGUE   FIGWORT FAMILY
(Penstemon)

From the Greek word 'pente' for five and 'stemon' for stamen, this showy flower grows throughout the west on dry slopes and in the pine-juniper forest. In the Grand Canyon National Park there are five different species ranging in color from pink to purple with slender leaves, opposite. On some species the upper leaves grow together. The irregular flowers are long, colorful tubular-shaped clusters at the top of a 2' high, erect stem. Indians used the red penstemon as a wash for burns and sores as it relieved pain.

SEGO LILY / MARIPOSA LILY   LILY FAMILY
(Calochortus Nuttallii)

"Calochortus' is a Greek word meaning a beautiful herb. 'Sego' is of Shoshone Indian origin. The creamy white petals with purple centers, either blotched or lined, is a tulip-shaped flower. There are from two - four blossoms on a single, erect, stiff stem about 1' high. The leaves are long, slender, almost grass like and rolled inward. Indians roasted and ate the onion-like bulbs which taste like potatoes when cooked. The delicate and beautiful lilies are found on dry mesa areas or in open mountain forests.

HORSEMINT / BERGAMOT   MINT FAMILY
(Monarda)

The reddish-purple, 4" stems are square with long purple flowers clustered at the head. Flowers are tubular with two lips. The almost triangular leaves grow opposite, and have toothed edges. They have a mint-like odor.

The white flowered horsemint *(Monarda pectinata)* grows in sandy soil on the South Rim of Grand Canyon. These flowers grow along the stem at the base of the leaf. Hopi Indians cultivate this herb and dry it for winter use.

128

LOCOWEED / MILKVETCH / RATTLEWEED   PEA FAMILY
(Astragalus oophorus)
    This is a spectacular blooming shrub which has a single purple flower on long stalks. The alternate leaves have many-paired leaflets. The fruit is a pod that is sausage-shaped about 1"-1½" long; red-brown, and when dry they can be rattled. Thus the name of 'rattleweed'. Some species are poisonous to horses and other livestock which causes a deadly loco disease. However, it is eaten by mice and other small animals as well as butterflies.

BUFFALO GOURD / CALABAZILLA   GOURD FAMILY
(Cucurbita foetidissima)
    A trailing, coarse, strong smelling plant with stems up to 15' high seen along roadsides with their yellow trumpet-shaped flowers. The alternating large, 12" wide hairy leaves are gray-green with cream-white stripes. The egg-shaped ball fruit is green striped, about 3"-4" in diameter. Roots are tubular. Found in sandy and gravelly places.

SUMMER TO FALL FLOWERS

SAGEBRUSH   SUNFLOWER FAMILY
(Artemisia tridentata)
    Found in deep, alkali-free soil, this widespread, very common desert shrub has a tangy, pungent aromatic odor and grows up to 4'-5' depending on the soil. The small, greenish yellow flowers are elongated clusters on a purplish, shaggy bark. This species has a three-toothed slender, silvery leaf. The foliage provides a good nesting place for sparrows and vireos. Rodents and deer eat the seeds.

SNAKEWEED   SUNFLOWER
(Gutierrezia sarothrae)
    The numerous, slender stems ending in a yellow ray of flowers form a low bushy plant seen on dry, rocky, open desert and mesa lands. Similar to the rabbit bush, only much smaller. Flowers are many, flat-topped, small heads that are narrow and pointed. Narrow, slender leaves grow alternately on the many stems of the branches. Navajo Indians use the snakeweed for a yellow dye.

RABBIT BUSH   SUNFLOWER FAMILY
(Chrysothamnus nauseosus)
    Found on arid slopes in open areas throughout the Grand Canyon country, it is a common silvery-green desert shrub. The bright, yellow, distinctive, fragrant flowers produces a white, downy seed in the autumn. The tough, straight, broom-like branches have many stems, and many flowers arranged in a flat 1"-2" topped cluster. Alternating leaves are long and narrow. Hopi and Navajo Indians use the flowers for yellow dye, and the inner bark for a green dye. It is useful for fuel and for wickerwork.

WILD CHRYSANTHEMUM   SUNFLOWER FAMILY
(Bahia dissecta)

A common yellow flower found in the pine-juniper forests and grassland country. The stout branches are topped with a group of flowers in petal-like rays surrounding the large centers. Grows to 3' high from the deep green 3-lobed basal leaves that are alternating. Each lobe has three divisions. Found on both rims in Grand Canyon National Park and Wupatki and Walnut Canyon National Monument.

AMARANTH   AMARANTH FAMILY
(Amaranthus)

Named from the Greek work for 'unfading' or 'incorruptible', this small desert plant has a pleasant fragrance. Also known as pigweed, it is found on dry, graveled slopes. There are many narrow leaves on the long slender stems. Blossoms are in dense spikes with yellow flowers extending under three bracts. Indians gathered the young plants for greens as the delicate taste is complimented with the stronger flavored mustard greens they also ate. The black, rounded seeds are eaten by mourning doves, finches, and sparrows as well as Indians. Seeds were also roasted or ground into flour.

WILD HELIOTROPE   WATERLEAF FAMILY
(Phacelia corrugata)

Also referred to as 'scorpionweed' as the curling of the blue flower heads resemble the striking position of a scorpion. Can be seen in the pinyon-juniper forest areas, especially along the South Kaibab and Bright Angel Trails, as well as on the North Rim. The striking bell-shaped flowers are on one side of the curling spike. Flowers are sweet smelling, although the plant exudes an onion-like odor. The purplish, hairy stems are branched with alternating, unequal lobes that are rounded. Another species that is common at Wupatki and Montezuma Castle National Monuments has deeper purple petals and cleft leaves.

FLOWERS BLOOMING FROM SPRING TO AUTUMN

VIGUIERA   SUNFLOWER FAMILY
(Viguiera multiflora)

A perennial herb found on both rims of the Grand Canyon in the pine-juniper forest. The several erect, slender stems have dark green, dotted, narrow, alternating leaves from 1"-2" long. The bright yellow flower heads are few, formed in a loose cluster with petal-like rays overlapping one another. The darker yellow center is tinged with brown and as the plant matures it becomes quite cone-shaped.

BABY ASTER *(Aster hirtifolius)*   SUNFLOWER FAMILY

HEATH-LEAVED ASTER *(Aster arenosus)*

Two common asters are found in Grand Canyon country on dry, rocky slopes, and along the trail. Blooms white then fades to pink or purple. Ray flowers about 7" wide appear at the head of the many branched stems that are slender on the woody base. The small numerous leaves that crowd the stems are alternating and hairy.

LUPINE
PEA FAMILY
(Lupinus palmeri)

The many varieties of the long-blooming lupine are found throughout the west decorating open fields, meadows, and slopes. Lupine is from the latin word 'lupus' meaning wolf, as the ancient belief was the plant preyed on and robbed the soil of goodness. The flowers are usually blue or violet, crowded together, whorling around the upper part of the stem. Alternating, palmate leaves are silver-green, divided into leaflets, radiating from a center. Commonly seen in the Grand Canyon country. Indians made a tea from the seeds as they found the plant medicinally beneficial.

WILD GERANIUM
(Geranium caespitosum)

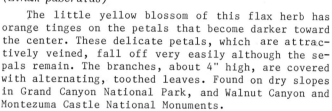

This showy white to pink flower, about 1" across has five petals with deep red to purplish veins, and curve downward; five sepals; and ten stamens. One or two stems emerge from a strong taproot, and stands erect up to 2' high. The leaves are hairy, 2"-4" long; are paired on long stems each, and palmately lobed into five to seven segments. Found in the pine forests, meadows, and sagebrush desert lands throughout the west, wherever there is rich, deep soil.

YELLOW FLAX
FLAX FAMILY
(Linum puberulus)

The little yellow blossom of this flax herb has orange tinges on the petals that become darker toward the center. These delicate petals, which are attractively veined, fall off very easily although the sepals remain. The branches, about 4" high, are covered with alternating, toothed leaves. Found on dry slopes in Grand Canyon National Park, and Walnut Canyon and Montezuma Castle National Monuments.

BLUE FLAX/PRAIRIE FLAX
(Linum lewisi)

The blue flax can be seen along the road on the North Rim. This 1'-3' high herb was named for Capt. Meriwether Lewis, of the famed Lewis and Clark Expedition. The many branched stems grow erect from a woody root base. Leaves are smooth, unlike the yellow flax. Seeds have a pleasing taste as well as being very nutritious. Indians used the fibrous plant for string. Early pioneers and Indians used this plant for medicinal purposes.

ROCKY MOUNTAIN BEEPLANT
CAPER FAMILY
(Cleome serrulata)

This is a lovely, delicate flower that beautifies the land of Antelope Valley and Navajo Indian Reservation on dry rocky shoulders. The plant stands from 2'-4' high with erect, slender, many branched stems. Each smooth leaf has three greenish-blue leaflets. As they have an unattractive odor when crushed, the plant is referred to as 'skunkweed'. The pink-purple, single flower of sepals united at the base of the clustered head, has four oblong petals. The delicate six long stamens are tipped with green and the anthers curl up. Seed pods hang down below the flower head which is found to be excellent nectar for honey.

APACHE PLUME   ROSE FAMILY
(Fallugia paradoxa)

With five white petals and many yellow stamens,
this member of the rose family is quite similar to
the cliff rose. However, it is a much smaller shrub
with fewer blossoms, that are larger in size. Seen
throughout the Grand Canyon country on dry mesas and
gullies. Flowers grow at the end of long white woody
branches that grow up to 5' high. In the fall the
fruit produces puffy seed balls of purplish-pink that
remain on the bush for a long period of time. The
bark is flaky. The five-parted deciduous leaves are
quite pronounced and have hairs.

INDIAN PAINTBRUSH   FIGWORT FAMILY
(Castilleja)

A beautiful, popular herb found all over the west
in dry, bushy slopes or along the road in deserts and
mountain regions. In the higher elevations, flowers
are more visible than those in the lower mesa regions
as they are practically covered by the bracts. Bracts
form a clustered 'brush' surrounding the flower at
the top of the stem. Colors vary from yellow, orange,
red or a deep red. Petals are green. This perennial
herb grows from a woody root-crown. Species differ in
their leaf formation as a single, alternating,
slightly leaf are on some, while others have narrower
leaves, or are three-lobed. The Hopi Indians use the
Indian paintbrush in their ceremonies.

WHITE CLEMATIS   BUTTERCUP FAMILY
(Clematis ligusticifolia)

Referred to by some as the 'traveler's joy', this
woody-type vine herb clings and covers fences, bushes
and rocks along streams or in damp places in a most
picturesque way. The small flowers, about ½" wide,
have no petals, only four sepals, and grow in branched clusters. The female flower produces plumed seeds
and grows separately from the male flower, which produces feathery stamens. The leaves are opposite, with
five to seven leaflets arranged on a leaf-stalk, that
appear almost like separate leaves. They are thick
and coarsely toothed. Found in Grand Canyon National
Park, and Montezuma Castle, Navajo, and Walnut Canyon
National Monuments.

ROTHROCK THISTLE   SUNFLOWER FAMILY
(Cirsium Rothrockii)

The rose-colored thistle is found along the road
of both the North and South Rims, and on dry, rocky
slopes. This species have spine-tipped leaves that
are not as fuzzy as the common purple thistle found
throughout the west. The crowded flower heads have
leafy bracts.

YELLOW-CENTERED THISTLE
(Cirsium ochrocentrum)

Also found on dry slopes and in the pine-juniper
forest. This thistle grows from a perennial base to
over 20" high with a stout stem covered with short,
densely matted white hairs. The barbes have long yellowish spines with the flowering cluster head at the
top of the branch.

THISTLE POPPY
(Argemone platyceras)

POPPY FAMILY

Known for its prickly stems and beautiful white flower with bright orange-yellow stamens, it is seen growing profusely on the Kaibab Plateau, House Rock Valley, and other open cattle country. The delicate, thin six petals are separated. The plant has several flower heads that measure from $2\frac{1}{2}$"-5" across. Stems grow up to 3' high. The buds and fruit have spiny horns. Alternate leaves are prickly and lobed.

DATURA/JIMSON WEED
(Datura meteloides)

POTATO FAMILY

A common roadside vine-like plant that spreads all over the ground in the pine-juniper forest and in the lower, open desert regions. Although referred to as the 'moon lily', it is not a lily, as the flower opens in the evening and closes by noon the following day. The large, white, funnel-shaped flowers are tinged with purple. The large gray-green leaves are coarsely toothed, and alternating. The fruit is a light brown, round pod, with short, thick prickles about the size of a walnut. It is a poisonous plant.

SUNFLOWER
(Helianthus)

SUNFLOWER FAMILY

This common yellow flower with many varieties throughout the Grand Canyon country, and the entire United States, grows from 3'-6' high in sandy soil. The large, yellow petal-rays encircle the purplish brown to deep brown center. The flower heads extend from 3"-6" across. The dull green, large 6" long, toothed, alternating, heart-shaped are on a many branched, sturdy, hairy, coarse stem.

The uses for this plant is as varied as the number of varieties. A yellow dye is made from the flowers. Purple and black dyes are made from the seeds. Hopi Indians use the dye for basketry, body decoration, and in the weaving of ceremonial blankets and robes. Roasted seeds are tasty, and are rich in proteins, vitamins, and minerals. Indians used seed oil to grease their hair, or grounded the seeds for flour. Roots have medicinal benefits and stalks yield a good fiber for making mats and nets. Bees make a good honey from the flowers. Birds and wild game eat the seeds. A sunflower muffin can be made from the ground seeds (1/3 cup) mixed with 1 cup each of white and whole wheat flour, 2 teaspoons of baking powder, 1/3 cup of brown sugar, $\frac{1}{2}$ cup milk, $\frac{1}{2}$ cup sour cream. Bake in muffin tins, 375° oven for 25 to 30 minutes.

GOLDENWEED
(Haplopappus gracilis)

SUNFLOWER FAMILY

Another yellow blooming flower referred to as 'yellow daisy', 'jimmyweed' or 'goldenbush'. It is a weedy, hairy plant growing on dry mesas, canyons, or rocky slopes in desert or in the pine-juniper forest. It grows up to 18" with many slender branches from a single root. The bright yellow ray flowers, and the center tubular ones, are formed above cup-shaped bracts. The narrow, alternating leaves have white tipped lobes.

SERVICE BERRY   ROSE FAMILY
(*Amelanchier utahensis*)

    This small, erect, deciduous shrub with brown branches is found on dry, rocky slopes or mesas among pinyon pines and sagebrush. It is an early flowering shrub with five white petals in a group of four to six, about 1", in a cluster. The toothed, simple ovate, alternating leaf is thin with a lighter undercoat and is somewhat hairy. The deep purple fruit is apple-like, round, with the upper flower tube still attached. Indians use the fruit dried and ground with meat, as well as for medicinal purposes. Songbirds and small animals like the sweet, juicy fruit and the larger animals such as deer and elk browse on the twigs and leaves.

SNOWBERRY   HONEYSUCKLE FAMILY
(*Symphoricarpos acutus*)

    An erect, deciduous shrub with white or pink bell-shaped flowers about 1½" long in an auxillary cluster, on slender branches. Berries are snowy-white waxy and round that contain two seeds each, and are eaten by birds. The thin, oval or round leaves are opposite, smooth with a bluish-green color above and a lighter shade underneath.

YUCCA / SOAPWEED / SPANISH BAYONET   LILY FAMILY
(*Yucca baccata*)

    About 30 broad, stiff bayonet-type, long pointed leaves with spiny tips form a dense basal rosette. They are a green or grayish-blue color. The central flowering stalk is plume-like with numerous waxy, cup-shaped creamy white or purple flowers in a bunch like bananas. The blossoms are fragrant and open at night. Flower clusters bloom from spring to summer. Black seeds in the pods are compressed. The plant is pollinated by the night-flying pronuba moth which lays eggs in the flower's ovary and in turn the larvae feed on the flat-winged seeds from the fruiting pods. The yucca and the moth could not survive without each other. It is interesting that such a forbidding plant can have so many uses. Each part supplies the Indian with something special. Young stalks, flowers, fruits, and seeds are food. Stalk fibers are used for making thread, brooms, blankets, and sandals. The sharp spikes of the leaves make excellent needles, and the root is used for a soap called 'amole' which the Hopi Indians use in their wedding ceremonies.

DWARF ASH   OLIVE FAMILY
(*Fraximus anomala*)

    A small tree-like shrub growing to about 15'-20' high that is known as the singleleaf ash. It is a very common deciduous tree found in the pinyon-juniper forest or in dry canyons and gulches. Branches have a smooth, dark brown bark with a tinge of red. The smooth, simple, slightly rounded leathery leaf is dark green above and paler green below. In the early spring the petalless green blossoms are orange. Fruit is about 1" long, rather flat and rounded with terminal wings.

TREES

UTAH JUNIPER
TAXODIUM FAMILY
(Juniperus osteosperma var. utahensis)

   Closely related to the cypress tree, this aromatic evergreen found in the Grand Canyon country is a small tree growing up to 15' high. The short, single main trunk has low, stiff branches to form a round crown. The bark is thin with the leaves shredded in circles. These scale-like leaves are small and sharply pointed. Cones appear at the end of the branches and are berry-like. The fruit is reddish-brown with berries being a fibrous, dry pulp and not juicy as in the other species of junipers.

JUNIPER MISTLETOE
MISTLETOE FAMILY
(Phoradendron juniperinum)

   Mistletoe is a parasitical plant growing on the junipers in the Grand Canyon country. It has scaly leaves and pearl-white berries on fragile, jointed, 1' long, olive-green stems that are easily broken. The strength of the tree can be sapped and eventually killed with over-infestation. Male and female plants grow separately. Hopi Indians use the plant for medicinal purposes.

PINYON PINE
PINE FAMILY
(Pinus edulis)

   Living in the same forest and desert mesa communities as the juniper, the pinyon pine grows up to 25" high with a round crown, and from 12"-15" in diameter. The bark is reddish-brown and irregularly furrowed with scales. The stiff needles are two in a bundle, and short. The cones, almost round, are 3" wide. The pinyon pine plays an important part in the life habits of the Indians. The profusion of large oily nuts from the cones ripen in the fall. They are pounded and ground into flour for cakes or cooked as mush, as the nuts are rich in protein. Indians used the gummy resin for waterproofing their baskets and pots, and as an adhesive for their jewelry. It was chewed as a gum, and applied to sores and burns. Pine nuts are sold commercially today as they are tasty raw, mixed in a salad, or cooked with vegetables.

PINE MISTLETOE
(Arceuthobium campylopodum)

   This mistletoe lives off the pine and fir trees. The leaves are yellow or brown and the berries are flatter than the juniper variety. Seeds are spread by birds from tree to tree.

GAMBEL'S OAK
BEECH FAMILY
(Quercus Gambeli)

   A common deciduous small tree that lives in cool mountain regions that is found in the pine-juniper forest communities. This bushy tree grows up to 50' high with male and female flowers appearing on the same tree. The gray bark is flaky. Leaves have distinctive lobes about 3"-6" long, and is unlike any other oak leaf. Acorns are half-covered with caps and is a good source of food for small animals and birds. Leaves as well as acorns are eaten by deer.

135

ENGELMANN SPRUCE   PINE FAMILY
(Picea Engelmannii)

This stately spruce grows in stands prominently in the Kaibab National Forest and on the North Rim in shady places which has deep rich soil with high moisture content. It is a cone-bearing evergreen with a single bluish-green, sharp, blunt needle that is soft and flexible, and curved toward the upper edge of the twig. Needles are square. The small twigs are light brown. Cones are not over 2½" long, with thin wedged-shaped scales of 1½", resembling those of the blue spruce. Cones appear in August and drop later in the autumn and winter. Some trees grow up to a great height with the old bark becoming very scaly. The thin outer layer of bark is reddish-brown with loosely attached scales. The crown of the tree is symmetrical and narrow with the lower branches drooping.

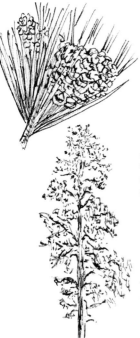

PONDEROSA PINE – WESTERN YELLOW PINE   PINE FAMILY
(Pinus ponderosa)

With a smooth, cylindral trunk, growing to over 170' to a narrow, spire-like crown, it is found on both rims of the Grand Canyon and other forest lands of northern Arizona. The root system is shallow and wide spreading with limbs short and stiff, turned upwards at the ends. Cones are oval shaped, clustered near the end of the branches. Needles are in bundles of three to five from 5"-11" long, deep yellow-green and grouped in heavy brush-like clusters at the end of the branch. The bark is 3"-4" thick and smells like vanilla with the yellow surface divided into the shield-like broad plates broken into small concave, flaky scales. The pitch from the bark is gummy and was used by the Indians as an adherant. Many small animals receive their shelter from the foliage and food from the leaves, bark and seeds.

DOUGLAS FIR   PINE FAMILY
(Pseudotsuga Menziesii)

On the North Rim these slender, slightly rounded and narrow crown evergreens grow in well-drained, humid places. They have graceful long sweeping, crowded branches. The strong roots provide substantial support for the tree. Bark is deeply furrowed of thick reddish-brown ridges. The single greenish-blue needle is flat and flexible growing around the branch. The oval, reddish-brown, 2" long cones hang down and fall soon after maturity. The female cone has prominent three-pronged bracts slightly longer than the scales. Male cones on the same tree are bright red and fall soon after the pollen is shed.

FREMONT COTTONWOOD   WILLOW FAMILY
(Populus Fremontii)

Growing along creeks, these graceful trees create welcome shade along the Bright Angel Trail at Indian Garden, on the North Kaibab Trail at Cottonwood Campground, at Phantom Ranch, and along Oak Creek. They grow to a height of 50'-100' with a spreading round crown. Trunks can be up to 4' in diameter with furrowed, whitish to gray-brown bark. Twigs are stout. Flowers of dense drooping catkins bloom in the spring before the leaves appear. The bright lustrous green leaves are triangular, heart-shaped from 2"-4" wide, flat, with round uneven toothed edges. The female species have seeds with long white silky hairs.

QUAKING ASPEN   WILLOW FAMILY
(Populus tremuloides)

In the autumn, these trees come into their own special glory when they present a great show of yellow or golden masses on mountain slopes and meadows. These slender tall trees are found in groves along streams, wet slopes and meadows in great profusion on the North Rim and in the Kaibab National Forest. Their slim greenish-white trunks, with horizontal markings and scars, grow up to a height of 20'-40'. The 1"-2" leaves are flat, wide, and ovate with a somewhat sharp point extending from a long stem. The light green leaves have a silvery-white undercoat and wave or flutter in the slightest breeze. Elk eat the leaves and beavers eat the bark as one of their staple foods. The small seeds scatter so far and wide that germination is rare, so new shoots sprout from the roots of the trees to produce new trees.

MESQUITE   PEA FAMILY
(Prosopis juliflora)

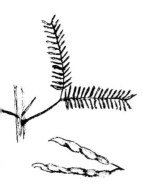

This large handsome shrub or small tree which grows up to 25' high in ideal conditions is commonly found in the desert along streams and washes. Roots extend to a depth of some 60' with more of the tree below the surface than above ground. The minute catkin-like greenish-yellow flowers are in long slender spikes, blooming from April to June. Insects and bees are attracted to their sweet fragrance. The flat yellow fruit pods, looking like string beans as they hang 2"-6" long, ripen in the fall. The numerous arched branches have straight sturdy thorns, and the bright green fern-type leaves are forked with many small leaflets. It is a good, long-lasting firewood used commercially today for barbeques, as the smoke from the coals enhance the flavor of the food.

IRONWOOD   PEA FAMILY
(Olneya tesota)

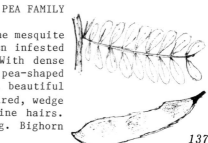

Growing in desert washes along with the mesquite and paloverde trees, the ironwood is often infested with mistletoe which stunts its growth. With dense evergreen foliage and wisteria-like purple pea-shaped flowers appearing in late spring, it is a beautiful tree. Fruit pods are hairy. Leaves are paired, wedge shaped, grayish-green and covered with fine hairs. The individual leaflets are about 1" long. Bighorn sheep and deer browse on the leaves.

137

WHERE TO WRITE

GRAND CANYON NATIONAL PARK
Grand Canyon, AZ., 86023

BACKCOUNTRY RESERVATION OFFICE
P.O.Box 129

BRIGHT ANGEL TRANSPORTATION DESK
Bright Angel Lodge

GRAND CANYON NATIONAL PARK LODGES
P.O.Box 699

FRED HARVEY, INC.
P.O.Box 507

GRAND CANYON LODGE (North
TWA Services, Inc.
P.O.Box TWA
Cedar City, Utah, 84720

KAIBAB NATIONAL FOREST - North
P.O.Box 248, Fredonia, AZ., 86022

KAIBAB NATIONAL FOREST - South
800 S. 6th St.
Williams, AZ., 86046

COCONINO NATIONAL FOREST
2323 E. Greenlaw Lane
Flagstaff, AZ., 86001

ARIZONA STATE PARKS
1688 West Adams
PHoenix, AZ., 85007

FLAGSTAFF CHAMBER OF COMMERCE
101 W. Santa Fe
Flagstaff, Az., 86001

GLEN CANYON NATIONAL RECREATIONAL
Box 1507, Page, AZ., 86040   AREA

GRAND CANYON CAVERNS
Peach Springs, AZ., 86434

HOPI CULTURAL CENTER
P.O.Box 67, Second Mesa, AZ., 86043

JACOB LAKE INN
Jacob Lake, AZ., 86022

MONTEZUMA CASTLE NATIONAL MONUMENT
P.O.Box 219
Camp Verde, AZ., 86322

NAVAJO NATIONAL MONUMENT
HC 71, Box 3, Tonalea, AZ., 86044

PAGE-LAKE POWER CHAMBER OF
6 N. 7th Ave.   COMMERCE
Page, AZ., 86040

SEDONA CHAMBER OF COMMERCE
Forest Road and Hawy. 89A
Sedona, AZ., 86336

SOUTHWEST PARKS & MONUMENTS
221 Court, Tucson Az., 85701

WAHWEAP LODGE AND MARINA
P.O.Box 1597
Page, Az., 86040

WALNUT CANYON NATIONAL
          MONUMENT
Rte.1, Box 25
Flagstaff, AZ., 86001

WILLIAMS CHAMBER OF
          COMMERCE
820 W. Bill Williams Ave.
Williams Az., 86046

WUPATKI-SUNSET NATIONAL
          MONUMENTS
Tuba Star Route
Flagstaff, 86001

INDEX

Dean Clark

H

Halls Crossing, 107
Hance Canyon, 25
Hance Rapids, 36
Havasu Canyon, 64,68-71,115
Havasu Creek, 53,64,68-71
Havasu Falls, 64,69,71
Havasu Point, 65
Havasupai Indians, 14,31,90
Havasupai Indian Res. 24,69
Hermits Rest, 19,20,21,34,65
Hermits Trail, 14,20,34
Hite, 107
Honeymoon Trail, 56
Hoover Dam, 9,15
Hopi Cultural Center, 89,90,91
Hopi Culture and Crafts, 90-93
Hopi Indian Reservation, 88,89,96
Hopi Point, 20
Horseshoe Mesa, 25,36
House Rock Buffalo Ranch, 50,57,65
House Rock Valley, 53,61,65
Hovenweep National Monument, 12
Hualapai Canyon, 53,64,69,72
Hualapai Hilltop, 64,69,71
Humphrey's Peak, 76
Hurricane Cliffs, 53,54,64

I

Indian Garden, 20,28,31,35,109
Inner Canyon, 21,25,28,29,31

J

Jacob Lake, 10,43,52,53,57,65
Jerome, 72,84,85
Johnson Point, 60

K

Kachinas, 91-93
Kaibab Lodge, 52
Kaibab National Forest, 41-43,53,
    55,57,64,65,69,72,77,115
    116,121,125,136,137
Kaibab-Paiute Indian Reservation,
    53,56,64
Kaibab Plateau, 9,40,41,53,65,133
Kaibito, 88
Kanab Creek, 53,64
Kanab Plateau, 9,53,64
Kayenta, 89,96,97,100
Keams Canyon, 89,90
Keet Seel, 10,12,13,88,89,102
Ken Patrick Trail, 40,41,49
Kykotsmovi, 90,91

L

Lake Mead National Recreational
    Area, 53,64
Lake Powell, 24,53,88,104,106,111
Lava Falls Rapids, 54,68
Lee, John Doyle, 58
Lees Backbone, 60
Lees Ferry, 14,15,53,59,60,65,
    88,111
Lees Ferry Trails, 60,61
Lipan Point, 25
Little Colorado River, 27,53,65,
    68,72,88
Little Coyote Canyon, 69
Little Nankoweap Creek, 49
Long Mesa, 69
Lowell Observatory, 76
Lower Lake Mary, 84,85
Lukachukai, 96

Dean Clark

IN APPRECIATION

No publication of this nature can be developed by any one
person. Many people have contributed their time and thought in
helping me make this book as accurate and up-to-date as possible by checking the manuscript and maps, or by supplying photographs. I would like to express my appreciation for the efforts
of all individuals at this time, especially:

Grand Canyon National Park
    Karen Berggren
    Erni Escalante
    Dale Schmidt
    Butch Wilson and his Ranger Staff
    Carol Wilson

Grand Canyon Natural History Association
    Anita Davis
    Sandra Scott
    Linda R. Swickard

Donald Barnes
Regis Cassidy — Kaibab National Forest at Fredonia
John Cummings — Pipe Springs National Monument
Robert Emerson — Wupatki-Sunset Crater National Monuments
Jeff Frank — Pipe Springs National Monument
Alice Gilmore — Betatakin Arts and Crafts
Sam Henderson — Walnut Canyon National Monument
Reuben Honahnie — Wupatki-Sunset Crater National Monuments
Larry Lake — Western River Expeditions
John K. Loleit — Navajo National Monument
John Noberto — Navajo National Monument
Stan Paterson — Kaibito, Navajo Indian Reservation
Stanley Paher — Nevada Publications
Ken Perry — Grand Canyon Caverns
Lynn Phipps — Walnut Canyon National Monument
Jigger Warren of Sedona

Flagstaff Chamber of Commerce
Hopi Cultural Center at Second Mesa
Hopi Silver Craft Guild at Oraibi
Williams Chamber of Commerce

The photograph of Nankoweap Canyon country on page 51 was
taken by the U.S. Forest Service at 35,000' elevation.
The Indian art on pages 4,98,99 are from "Decorative Arts
of the Southwest Indians" by Dorothy S. Sides, Fine Arts Press.

A special heartfelt thanks to Connie Rudd of the National
Park Service for contributing so many beautiful photographs to
better portray this magnificent country. Notably the front and
back wrap-around cover and the inside back cover photographs.
My deep appreciation and thanks is also extended to MAC
and Dean Clark for assistance and the use of their photographs.

PUBLICATIONS BY LEW AND GINNY CLARK

YOSEMITE TRAILS

One of the best, most complete and informative, up-to-date books on the Park with 5-color USGS Topo and 4-color area maps, photographs, wildlife notes and trail profiles showing elevation and mileage between points by a former Park Ranger. 144 pages. $6.95

SEQUOIA-MT. WHITNEY TRAILS

A complete guide to the Park including the southern portion of the John Muir and Pacific Crest Trail. 5 and 4 color maps for both the eastern and western approaches to this magnificent wilderness. Wildlife notes, sketches and photographs. 80 pages. $5.95

KINGS CANYON COUNTRY

A companion book to 'Sequoia-Mt. Whitney Trails' in the same format covering the Park as well as the Shaver Lake and Huntington Lake area, Bishop Creek and eastern approaches to the John Muir Trail. 80 pages. $5.95

MAMMOTH-MONO COUNTRY

This is THE guide to the famous year-round resort area with multi-colored maps, sketches, photographs that includes June Lake, Rock Springs, and Mono Lake areas. Nature note and special winter section. 96 pages. $5.95

HIGH MOUNTAINS AND DEEP VALLEYS
The Gold Bonanza Days

The first book of its kind on the Basin and Range country that includes Death Valley, ghost towns from Calico to Virginia City, Owens Valley, Bristlecone Pine Forest, and eastern approaches to the Sierra. Sketches, photographs and maps. Interesting personal historical data. 192 pages. $6.95

SIERRA WILDFLOWER PRINT POSTALS

Twelve beautiful floral photographic prints in full color of favorite Sierra flowers to treasure or send to friend or give as a gift. Packaged. Set of 12 - $2.50